Return to Midway

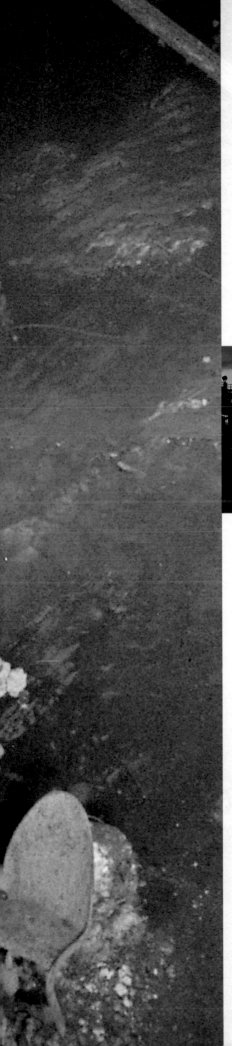

Return to Midway

Robert D. Ballard
and Rick Archbold

Principal photography by David Doubilet
Additional photography by Mark Thiessen,
Keith Morehead and Glen Marullo

Underwater paintings by Ken Marschall

Technical and historical consultation by Robert J. Cressman,
Charles Haberlein, Jr., and John Lundstrom

NATIONAL GEOGRAPHIC
WASHINGTON D.C.

A NATIONAL GEOGRAPHIC/MADISON PRESS BOOK

Design and compilation © 1999 Madison Publishing Inc.
Text © 1999 Odyssey Corporation and Rick Archbold

First published in the U.S.A. by
The National Geographic Society
1145 17th Street, N.W.
Washington, D.C. 20036-4688

1 2 3 4 5 6 7 8 9

Library of Congress Cataloging-in-Publication Data

Ballard, Robert D.
    Return to Midway : the quest to find the Yorktown and the other lost ships from the pivotal battle of the Pacific War / by Robert D. Ballard and Rick Archbold.
      p.   cm.
    Includes bibliographical references and index.
      ISBN 0-7922-7500-4
    1. Midway, Battle of, 1942. 2. Shipwrecks—Pacific Ocean.
    3. World War. 1939-1945—Naval operations, American.
      I. Archbold, Rick, 1950- . II. Title.
    D774.M5B35   1999
    940.54′26—dc21   99-10831
                      CIP

(Right) Midway-era American planes salute the modern American carrier *Constellation*.

Produced by
Madison Press Books
40 Madison Avenue
Toronto, Ontario
Canada M5R 2S1

Printed and bound in Great Britain

Contents

**(Left) Launching the Advanced Tethered
Vehicle (ATV) from the *Laney Chouest*.**

To the brave U.S. fliers and sailors who sacrificed their lives and turned the tide of war in the Pacific during the historic battle of Midway, June 4, 1942.

—Robert D. Ballard

Chapter One
Field of Battle

Saturday, May 2, 1998: Early Morning

I AWOKE AT 0430 AFTER A RESTLESS NIGHT AND LAY IN BED FOR AN HOUR, MY MIND turning over and over the many questions surrounding our Midway expedition. Finally I got out of my bunk and decided to write in my log. It passes the time and helps me focus.

We've been at sea only about two days, but already our world has closed in. It seems strange that in the midst of the vast, featureless Pacific, where you sometimes feel you can see almost as far as eternity, the limits of our existence have shrunk to the boundaries of our little ship, the *Laney Chouest*. Our lives are now contained by a vessel much smaller than a World War II destroyer and constrained by our mission—to explore the underwater vestiges of a great and famous battle.

In the whole history of naval warfare, there have been few to match it: Salamis, the defeat of the Spanish Armada, Trafalgar, Jutland. Before the Battle of Midway on June 4, 1942, the United States and its allies were on the run in the Pacific and the Japanese looked unstoppable. After Midway, the Japanese never again really took the offensive at sea. And when you think about the odds against an American victory—the incredible risk the Americans were taking and the overwhelming superiority of the Japanese forces—the result looks even more astonishing. The military historian John Keegan has called it "as great a reversal of strategic fortune as the naval world has ever seen."

No wonder there has been so much interest in our expedition and so much expectation attached to it. I would be happier if our mission was a secret until after we find our ships—five famous aircraft carriers and one destroyer. We have only four weeks to do this: Two weeks to find six shipwrecks, two weeks to explore them with

(Right) From the air, Midway, actually two islands, today looks quite different from the military base of 1942, when the airstrip was on the smaller Eastern Island. Now airplanes land only on the larger Sand Island, while Eastern is a wildlife refuge, its runways overgrown with vegetation.

remotely controlled still and video cameras. In the next 14 days, we hope to find both the American aircraft carrier *Yorktown* and the *Hammann*, the destroyer that went down with her with a terrible loss of life. If we are lucky, we may also come across some of the airplanes lost when the *Yorktown* sank. Then we plan to hunt down the four lost Japanese aircraft carriers, the *Akagi*, the *Hiryu*, the *Soryu*, and the *Kaga*.

The odds against finding even one of these ships look at least as long as the odds against an American victory almost 56 years ago. The sunken ships of Midway are deeper than any wrecks I've ever found. And every additional inch of depth complicates the matter of exploration: sonar provides less detail; each launch and recovery of a deep-towed vehicle takes more time; the possibility of equipment malfunction increases. I know from experience that even the most solid-seeming sinking positions usually turn out to be far from accurate. The confusion of battle keeps navigators busy, but not at calculating a precise fix. Look at the sinking of the *Bismarck*, for example. A whole fleet of British ships pounded her for hours, then watched her sink, yet she was miles from the official sinking position the British recorded. Our information on where the Japanese ships sank is, to put it mildly, sketchy. Finding even one of these lost ships would constitute a real victory. Nonetheless, I have to believe that we will prevail. Somehow. I can't let down all the people whose hopes are riding on this expedition, above all the four veterans on board. Finding the *Yorktown* will mean so much to the two Americans. And finding even one of the Japanese carriers will mean so much to the two Japanese sailing with us, especially if we find their ship, the *Kaga*.

I can't help wondering what's going through the minds of these two elderly gentlemen, both of them former members of the Japanese Imperial Navy's crack flying corps, or through the minds of the two American veterans of the battle who are also with us. So far the two Japanese have kept mostly to themselves, unable to communicate without the mediation of their young translator, Junko Taguchi, an attractive woman in her 30s. Yuji Akamatsu, a stocky fellow who looks like he has spent his life outdoors, appears to have a ready sense of humor. It's too bad I can't understand his jokes since he always seem to be laughing at something. He seems to defer to Haruo Yoshino, a taller and more formal gentleman. I notice that the translator defers to him, as well. She

Our base ship, the *Laney Chouest*, leaves Midway for the *Yorktown* search area. A former Louisiana oil rig tender, the *Laney*'s dynamic positioning system allows her to stay in one spot even in strong winds and currents, an invaluable feature when exploring sunken ships.

never speaks directly to Mr. Akamatsu but always to him through Mr. Yoshino.

The two Americans, Harry Ferrier and Bill Surgi, couldn't be more different—except that they both spent most of their adult lives in the United States Navy, Harry as an officer, Bill as an enlisted man. On June 4, 1942, Harry was a young radioman, barely old enough to have graduated from high school, when he climbed aboard his brand new TBF-1 torpedo bomber, or Avenger, sitting on a Midway runway to await the signal that the Japanese fleet had been sighted. He had never been in combat before. Nor had anyone else in his six-plane detachment, which would soon be taking part in an attack on the most seasoned striking force in the Japanese navy.

Bill was an aviation mechanic attached to the *Yorktown*'s fighter squadron, known as Fighting Three, commanded by the soon-to-be famous Jimmy Thach. Surgi experienced the Battle of Midway, as did most of its participants, at his battle station. He watched as the attacking enemy planes dodged the American fighters and then homed in on his ship. He felt the impact of each bomb and each torpedo that struck. He saw shipmates wounded and killed. He abandoned the ship he called home for a very

long swim in the Pacific while waiting to be rescued. I'm sure before the voyage is out that he and Mr. Akamatsu and Mr. Yoshino will have exchanged their stories of being aboard a carrier under attack. The two Japanese fliers were both back on board the *Kaga* when she was crippled by American dive-bombers. They both watched her sink. At least Bill Surgi was spared that final ignominy.

In just a few hours we will be on site, and our hunt for the *Yorktown* can begin. But the biggest question right now is whether the *Yorktown* is actually where we have decided to look for her—inside the search quadrant I've drawn on the Navy's spiffy new bathymetric chart, which records water depth at regular intervals, giving us the closest thing we've got to a topographical map of the ocean floor. Other questions also nag. Even if we're looking in the right place, will the wreck be visible to our instruments? We're looking for an object three miles deep—half a mile deeper than the place where we found the *Titanic*. And how will my team perform? Most of them have never been to sea with me before, never been tested against the inevitable mishaps of deep-ocean exploration. How will they hold up when things start to go wrong, as they always do? What about my own stamina? I'm not getting any younger, but the ships are just as hard to find. So many imponderables—as many as I've ever taken to sea at once.

For example, my expeditions have often been joint ventures with the U.S. Navy, but I have never worked with this particular team before. The Navy has lent us their Advanced Tethered Vehicle to be our video eyes on the ocean floor. Having the Navy along seems only appropriate as we explore one of the most glorious moments in its history. But I wonder how much this young Navy team knows or cares about the

The four veterans who joined our Midway expedition (from far left to far right): Bill Surgi, Harry Ferrier, Yuji Akamatsu, and Haruo Yoshino. What would they feel when they again saw the waters where friends had died half a century before?

Battle of Midway? I'll bet not much. Not yet. But by the end of the expedition, I'd be willing to wager that will have changed.

No one who has sailed with me in quest of a lost ship is ever quite the same afterward. For me, however hard the hunt, the discovery brings a kind of release, almost a mystic moment, which I guess I've become addicted to. When the search seems to go on forever, as it often does, and the food gets worse and spirits sag lower and lower, I often ask myself why I have made the hunt for sunken ships my particular passion. Why do I keep pitting myself against such long odds? After all the expeditions I have led, and all the shipwrecks I've found, you might think it would get easier. But it doesn't. Every time, fate throws the unexpected in the way. Every time, luck and instinct play as big a role as science and technology.

But the exploration game is more than a job, more than a quantifiable scientific challenge like the ones that used to occupy my days as a young oceanographer at the Woods Hole Oceanographic Institution. The moment of discovery—whether of the *Titanic* or of the *Bismarck* or of a Roman wreck that's almost two thousand years old—

(Below) Our search area for the *Yorktown* (above left) and the destroyer *Hammann* (above right) lay to the east and north of Midway Island. Since accounts differ on where the two ships sank, we had to cover a large area.

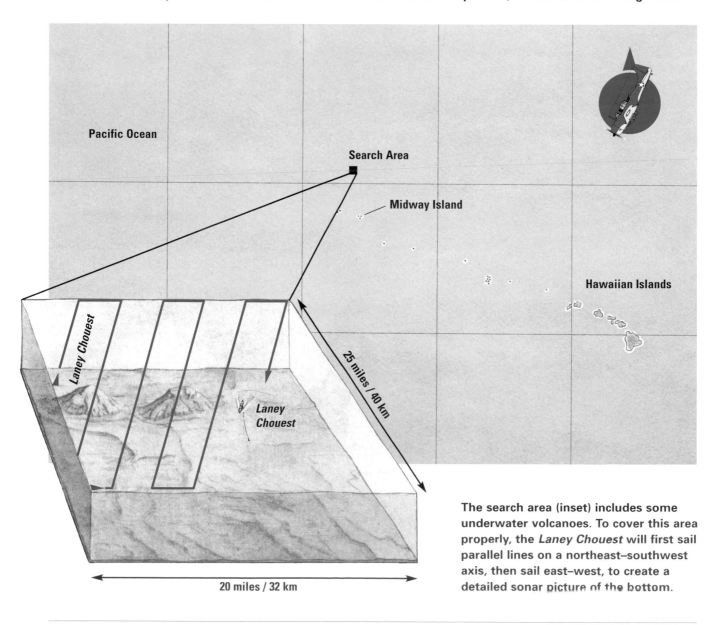

The search area (inset) includes some underwater volcanoes. To cover this area properly, the *Laney Chouest* will first sail parallel lines on a northeast–southwest axis, then sail east–west, to create a detailed sonar picture of the bottom.

opens a doorway into history. It brings the past into the present. When I peered through the *Titanic*'s portholes, I could almost hear the laughter, the music, feel the insouciance of a whole era heading straight for disaster. When—as I hope I will—I fly above the flight decks of the *Yorktown* or the *Kaga*, I will be back in the middle of a great battle. I'll be flying with Harry Ferrier or Yuji Akamatsu or Haruo Yoshino. There's no armchair substitute for that extraordinary feeling.

Like the mythical Greek explorer Jason, and his Argonauts, I'm willing to go to the ends of the earth in search of a golden fleece. Not that our ship, the *Laney Chouest*,

The *Laney Chouest* seen from astern. Our sonar, *MR-1* was launched from a track in the center of the stern. The starboard crane is for our Advanced Tethered Vehicle (ATV).

conjures up visions of a vessel as romantic as Jason's *Argo*. In fact it was never meant for mid-ocean voyaging. Its flat bottom, perfect for the vessel's intended role as an oil rig tender, makes us feel as if we're riding on a large raft with propellers. Fortunately the weather has been absolutely perfect: gentle winds and calm seas, much like the weather during the Battle of Midway. With any luck it will stay that way. I don't want our Midway veterans to face any more Pacific storms. When I first met them at the hotel in Honolulu a few days ago, I was struck by a strong sense that for them the late 20th century had already melted away. They had traveled back in time to their late teens or early 20s and were living in a forgotten world—a world at war. Except that the old hatreds were dead. These four old warriors—two Americans and two Japanese—were reliving an old battle, but they had no interest in refighting it. For me, however, the battle had just begun.

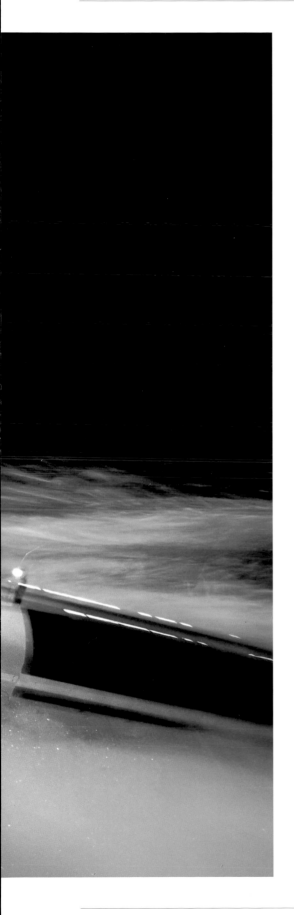

Saturday, May 2: Evening

WE NOW HAVE ONE DAY OF SEARCHING UNDER OUR BELTS. SO far, so good. We have run three search lines and the side-scan sonar vehicle—*MR-1*—seems to be working just fine. The team from the University of Hawaii are real pros. I'm very impressed. But I'm still worried.

No sooner had we launched *MR-1* than I was second-guessing my decision to use a high-altitude sonar to look for a wreck this deep. The sonar was designed—and is almost exclusively used—as a deep-ocean mapping machine that reveals the broad contours of undersea geography but leaves out the details. My doubts haven't been helped by talking to *MR-1*'s chief scientist, Bruce Appelgate. Bruce put the problem all too succinctly: "You're asking us to look for a needle in a haystack with a vehicle that's designed to look for haystacks." There's no question that searching for a deep wreck with a shallow-towed sonar is one of the biggest gambles I've ever taken, but it was simply the best system we could afford.

I've done the math, however, and in theory—in theory— *MR-1* should spot a *Yorktown*-size target if the ship sank in one piece. But only just. In three miles of water, it takes eight seconds for each ping the sonar sends out to travel from the vehicle to the bottom and back. Even if we tow the vehicle as slowly as we can before it begins to fishtail (about 3.5 knots), the roughly 800-foot length of the *Yorktown* would translate into 18 sonar hits—and that's assuming we are running perfectly along the ship's linear axis. On the sonar printout, those 18 hits would add up to a dark spot about the size and shape of a small grain of rice. At other angles, it will be even smaller—if we can see it at all.

Of course this all assumes a smooth, featureless bottom, what ocean geologists refer to as an abyssal plain. Yet the *Yorktown*'s generally accepted sinking position—the one arrived at by both the historian Adm. Samuel Eliot Morison and the experts at the Naval War College—places it right over a large underwater volcano, a submerged feature that forms part of the long chain of volcanoes

Bruce Appelgate watches *MR-1* being lowered from the *Laney Chouest*'s fantail. Towed at a shallow depth, the *MR-1* can be launched or recovered quickly—an advantage over deep-towed sonars during exploration.

responsible for the Hawaiian archipelago, of which Midway is an isolated part. In the peaks and valleys of these seamounts, a target as tiny as the *Yorktown* would disappear in the backscatter—the background of sonar noise—unless, like the *Bismarck*, it landed on a slope steep enough to launch a landslide much larger and longer than the ship itself. Our sonar would definitely pick up such a landslide.

I'm far from convinced that the *Yorktown* sank anywhere near the accepted spot. The historian on board, Chuck Haberlein of the Naval Historical Center in Washington, D.C., has made a painstaking analysis of all the available data on the battle, and he has come to a very different conclusion. Taking the logs of the several destroyers escorting the *Yorktown* the day before she sank, he has plotted all their estimated positions during the ship's final hours. With one notable exception, the destroyer *Benham*, a healthy number of these positions are clustered in a two- or three-square-mile area roughly ten miles to the south of Morison's fix. If it weren't for that one set of crazy positions, I'd be convinced that we will find the *Yorktown* in or near that cluster. Otherwise, I have never before had such good data to base a search area on. What's more, this data sends me to the south of the volcano, where the undersea terrain flattens out into a nice inviting abyssal plain. Perfect for Bruce's sonar.

The box I've drawn on the chart encloses both Morison's position to the north and the destroyer cluster to the south, a total area of 500 square miles—as much as the search areas for the *Bismarck* and the *Titanic* combined. As with the *Titanic*, I've had to factor in the current, which helped explain why that wreck was so far away from its distress position. From looking at the logs of the destroyers accompanying the *Yorktown* during its final hours, we have guessed the current was running at about half a knot to the south–southwest (bearing roughly 220°). After the *Yorktown*'s fatal torpedo hits, she remained afloat for 15 ½ hours. According to the destroyers' positions, I expect we will find the wreck about one mile southwest of the spot where she was when attacked by the Japanese submarine. If I draw a line between two of the destroyer sinking positions, they intersect the line of drift at a point just about a mile south–southwest—right where the *Yorktown* should be. Things then start to look pretty good.

But when I consider that three previous expeditions had failed to find the *Titanic* before we finally did, and that it took me two years to locate the *Bismarck*, my confidence starts to crumble. If the ship is near Morison's position, our only hope of finding it is to do a visual search for a debris trail or a landslide. The logical strategy, therefore, is to look to the south. Only when and if we don't find the ship in the flat-lands will we attempt any kind of foray into Morison's nasty-looking mountains.

WE HAD A BIT OF EXCITEMENT THIS MORNING WHEN OUR FIRST SONAR PASS THROUGH THE high-probability area identified what looked like a promising target. The promise evaporated when we passed by the position on our second line, this time at right angles to our previous line, and the target vanished. This incident graphically demonstrates the difference between a visual search with a deep-towed camera vehicle and a sonar search with a shallow-towed fish—the nickname we give to the bullet-shaped sonar emitter that's towed behind the ship. With the camera, what you see is what you get; with the sonar, what you see is what you get only if it looks the same from every angle.

For this phase of the expedition, the search phase, I will be spending most of my time in the ship's dry lab, which we've already nicknamed the War Room. It's right next to the wet lab, where the *MR-1* crew have set up their workstation—the

Dave Mindell of M.I.T. and I hunch over the light table in the War Room to examine the latest printout of sonar coverage of our search area.

computers that take the raw sonar data and turn it into images of the seafloor. The War Room is where I do my thinking and my plotting. A large chart of the search area sits on a light table that occupies most of the room. At my elbow usually sits a scale model of the *Yorktown*. (The model reminds me of what I'm looking for.) On the chart I've marked the Morison position and the various positions reported by the destroyers. A heavy pencil line defines the search quadrant. I've laid a large piece of Mylar over the chart. Every half hour we enter the latest satellite fix on the Mylar overlay. At the end of each sonar pass, we connect the dots to show our actual track line. Since *MR-1* has a blind spot about a mile wide directly beneath it, we have to be sure our coverage overlaps to eliminate all the gaps.

On a second sheet of Mylar, which I can lay on top of the first, I've begun to build a detailed picture of the ocean floor. This is where the *MR-1* team has really been strutting its stuff. Bruce Appelgate and his four-member group stand 12-hour watches. I don't know how they do it. Bruce, who's a young Ph.D. in marine geology and geophysics, serves as watch leader during the day. Karen Sender, who acts like everybody's older sister—she even wears funny fluffy purple slippers—takes the night shift. Karen likes nothing better than massaging raw sonar data into what she describes as "beautiful pictures of the seafloor." She's been around the *MR-1* since its invention. Before that she worked with *MR-1*'s predecessor *SeaMARC*. You might say she's a sonar junkie.

What one of Bruce and Karen's beautiful pictures consists of is a long strip of gray-looking paper that represents one sonar pass across our search area. That's what I place on my second Mylar overlay. As the coverage begins to overlap, so do these strips. I trim them with scissors, and eventually my cutouts make up a fairly detailed sonar picture of our search area.

It can be many hours before a real-time pass becomes one of these strips of paper, which means that most of the time nothing is happening. Today, while waiting, I pored over the action reports and ships' logs from those destroyers, looking for some new piece to the puzzle.

My sounding board and soul mate at times like these is Dave Mindell, a former junior scientist at Woods Hole's Deep Submergence Laboratory, who now teaches the history of technology at MIT. On this expedition, Dave is my alter ego. He's also my ambassador to the Navy techies on board. Dave is as comfortable getting his hands dirty replacing some burned-out circuitry as he is discussing the evolution of naval ordnance or wrestling with the question of where the *Yorktown* really sank. When the two of us confront a problem, we seem to be able to communicate without words. In a crisis his concentration is as ferocious as mine.

Today those oddball destroyer positions really had me mesmerized. I was determined to figure out why one set of positions should be so at odds with the rest. Maybe by solving this puzzle, I'd learn something more about where the *Yorktown* really was. My approach to a problem such as this is to go over and over the data, doing and redoing every calculation. Often I'll just sit and stare at the numbers, waiting for inspiration to strike. Today my inspiration was pure platinum. What if, I suddenly wondered, the enlisted man whose job was to type up the handwritten rough log on the *Benham* consistently misread certain numbers? I quickly made some calculations. If I started substituting some numbers for others, say eights for threes in the offbeat positions, they fell in with those from the rest of the destroyers. Bingo! I felt a little bit like a wartime code breaker squeezing secrets out of enemy gibberish.

So I'm going to bed more confident than ever that the *Yorktown* is inside my box and on level ground. But will *MR-1* see it?

Sunday, May 3

L AST NIGHT MY ANXIETY ALMOST REACHED A LEVEL OF PANIC OVER *MR-1*'S ABILITY to find the wreck. I lay awake for what seemed like hours, going over the numbers in my head. If the ship lies in the abyssal plain, if it's still in one piece, if the sonar is working perfectly, we should be able to find it. This is my third bad night's sleep in a row. If I keep this up, I won't be in a state to search for any wreck: I'll be a basket case before our first week is over.

At least the vets seem to be getting along famously. Today I watched for a while as Peter Schnall and his crew from Partisan Pictures filmed them reminiscing about the battle. It's not the first time I've marveled at meetings of old adversaries who inevitably find that much more now unites than divides them. One of the things they share is an intensity of experience inexplicable to those who have never been in battle. Such shared experience surely accounts for the friendships that have sprung up between men who once fought each other so bitterly.

(Above) Harry Ferrier pokes his finger through the bullet hole in the baseball cap he wore during the battle. (Below) Bill Surgi sits with the "tin hat" he saved from the abandoned *Yorktown*.

On June 4, 1942, Harry Ferrier barely escaped with his life during an air attack on the Japanese fleet. On our expedition, he has brought along a baseball cap he wore that day. The cap has a hole in it where a Japanese bullet grazed his skull. (Harry also salvaged a piece of his airplane, but he didn't bring that with him.) Bill Surgi has also brought along an item of headgear, the steel helmet he wore as part of *Yorktown*'s damage control crew and wouldn't part with when he abandoned ship. He refers to the helmet as his "tin hat." Our two Japanese veterans don't seem to have brought along any souvenirs. I guess they were too busy getting off the burning carrier *Kaga*. Both men were airborne on June 4. Yoshino commanded the lone scout plane launched from *Kaga*. Akamatsu flew on antisubmarine patrols.

The experiences of these four make any problems we might face seem pretty pale. The occasional equipment malfunction can't compare with the loss of a friend or a limb. But I can't help noting the parallels between their battle and ours. Our team is in many ways as untested as the Americans were in 1942. I don't know how we will measure up, how we will do when we confront our first real setback. Like the opposing forces at Midway, we will stand or fall on our ability to adapt to changing fortunes, to make the right decision when something doesn't go our way in the heat and haze of battle. Luck as well as skill will play a big part in our ultimate triumph or defeat.

Victory. Defeat. Those words had very different connotations for the Japanese and Americans at the beginning of June 1942. Since the surprise attack on Pearl Harbor on December 7, 1941, the Japanese Navy had swept eastward across the Pacific and southward through the Philippines and Southeast Asia into the Indian Ocean as remorselessly as Hitler's panzers had swept through Europe in the early days of the war. Victory was almost all they knew. Between February and April 1942 the Americans had managed a series of successful raids on Japanese bases, but only at the Battle of the Coral Sea had they begun to compensate for their humiliation at Pearl Harbor. Yet with only three

(Left) Comdr. Kurt Sadorf, head of the navy team, drops a transponder over the side. These sonar beacons will serve as reference points for tracking the ATV in the search area and enable us to return precisely to the location of a promising target.

(Above) Yuji Akamatsu and Haruo Yoshino share a contemplative moment. (Opposite) This view of *MR-1* shows the winch drum for raising and lowering the sonar vehicle.

aircraft carriers operating in the vast Pacific theater at this time, the Pacific fleet was badly overextended. Many Americans believed that sooner or later the Japanese fleet would successfully land troops on the U.S. West Coast.

Not even the most far-fetched of Japanese plans included an invasion of the American mainland, however. Midway made some sense as a piece of the defensive perimeter of their Greater East Asian Co-Prosperity Sphere, the Pacific empire they hoped to build. In fact Midway was farther than almost everyone except Adm. Isoroku Yamamoto wanted to go, although an eventual occupation of Hawaii was always a possibility. He believed that the occupation of Midway would entice the much weaker American fleet into a decisive battle that Japan would win. If he could defeat the United States at Midway, he reasoned, the Americans might be willing to concede control of the western Pacific to Japan. In a long war, as Yamamoto knew from his own visits to America, the more populous and industrially more powerful United States would ultimately prevail.

There was no room for error on this operation. If the Japanese didn't win at Midway and win big, the emperor didn't stand a chance.

Monday, May 4

ANOTHER DAY SPENT "MOWING THE LAWN," OUR NAME FOR THE BACK-AND-FORTH course the ship follows during our sonar search. Already the tense boredom so common on this sort of expedition has begun to set in. It's interesting to see how different people cope. Some, like Bill Surgi, fill their downtime with projects. Others, like Harry Ferrier, become more withdrawn, more contemplative. Still others, like me, tend to stew. And stew.

It's easy to forget that most exploration, most of the time, means drudgery. It's only in retrospect that the process of discovery looks romantic. Yet exploration feeds the human soul in some profound way. It must feed mine. How else to explain why I keep coming back for more?

To explore means to search for something bigger than yourself. It means measuring yourself against challenges that are both physical and mental. The need to explore the frontier, whatever that may be at a given moment in history, is fundamental to the human experience. Would I sign on for the first trip to Mars? In a heartbeat. Would I scale Mount Everest if I physically could? Absolutely. It just happens that the deep ocean is my frontier and that looking for shipwrecks is what I know how to do.

Tuesday, May 5

AVE MINDELL HAS JUST POKED HIS HEAD INTO MY CABIN TO tell me that our Advanced Tethered Vehicle (ATV) suffered a major ground short when it reached 5,000 feet and is being recovered. The Navy estimates that fixing it will take 24 hours. It's almost midnight, but I'm wide awake, which is why I'm making this entry in my personal log.

This morning, after we spent four days mowing the lawn, our initial sonar survey of the primary *Yorktown* search area was completed, all 500 square miles of it, including the mountains to the north. While I didn't expect the sonar to see the ship in such rough terrain, it would have detected a landslide similar to the one caused by the *Bismarck*. We had covered the whole 500-square-mile area fairly thoroughly, running a second set of east–west lines at right angles to our original coverage north–south. Our cut-and-paste sonar mosaic of the ocean floor sits complete on the light table in the War Room. But where is the *Yorktown*? Each sonar picture shows a fair number of targets that could be an aircraft carrier. They might just as easily be hunks of rock. The only way we'll find out for sure is to put the ATV in the water.

(Above) Cathy Offinger and I ponder the chart of the search area. The sonar mapping gave us only a selection of probable targets. But which, of any of these, would prove to be the *Yorktown?* Once we had determined our most likely targets, we would use the navy's ATV (opposite) to get a better look at them. (Below) A night launch of the ATV.

Since no single target leaps out at us—there are a couple that look particularly promising—I've decided to conduct a visual search in our highest probability area. Which means towing our robot video back and forth across the ocean floor at right angles to the axis of the underwater current. Which means we're back to the strategy that found the *Titanic*. All ships drop debris as they sink, leaving a trail on the bottom. The deeper the water, the more spread out the trail. At a depth of three miles, that debris trail ought to be at least a mile long.

With the *Titanic*, one of the ship's boilers led us to the wreck. With the *Yorktown*, maybe it will be an antiaircraft gun or a piece of a Grumman F4F-4, or Wildcat, fighter.

With the ATV out of commission, that plan is in ruins. Now that I'm awake, I think I'll stroll down to the wet lab to see how the *MR-1* night watch is doing. Maybe Karen Sender and Nathan Becker, the University of Hawaii grad student working as data tech on the night shift, have found something that the rest of us have missed.

I can't help but note to myself, as our Midway expedition enters this critical phase, that we are groping in the dark as much as the opposing fleets that approached each other during the long night of June 3–4, 1942. I don't imagine Bill Surgi, Harry Ferrier, Yuji Akamatsu, or Haruo Yoshino slept too well on the eve of the battle. I don't imagine they are sleeping all that soundly as they return to Midway.

The surprise Japanese attack on Pearl Harbor at dawn on December 7, 1941, seriously damaged eight battleships, sinking four, including the *Arizona* (above), which with the other big-gun ships of the Pacific fleet was moored on Battleship Row (below left). Today the submerged *Arizona* is the centerpiece of the Pearl Harbor war memorial. (Below right) Her magazines hit, the destroyer *Shaw* blew up in drydock. (Globe, opposite) After Pearl Harbor, the Japanese navy swept decisively east and south across the Pacific.

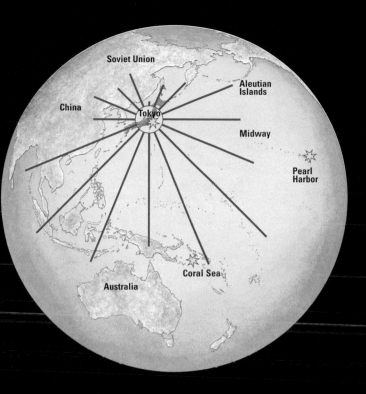

Turning the Tide

As stunning as it was for the United States, the Japanese attack on Pearl Harbor on December 7, 1941, was more a psychological setback than military defeat. Although 18 ships were sunk or damaged, by a stroke of luck, all the Pacific fleet's aircraft carriers were at sea. As early as December 31, 1941, the psychological tide began to turn, when Adm. Chester Nimitz took over as commander in the Pacific. Under Nimitz's astute strategic leadership, the badly outmatched Pacific fleet made the most of its scarce resources, harrying the Japanese and slowing their advance.

The two adversaries did not meet head-to-head until the Battle of the Coral Sea in early May, when American and Japanese carriers squared off in the first-ever naval engagement fought exclusively by fleets of fighters and bombers. The Americans prevented the invasion of Port Moresby, New Guinea, while proving they could stand up to the best of the Japanese Imperial Navy. And so the stage was set—for Midway.

On April 18, 1942, sixteen Army B-25 bombers under the command of Gen. James Doolittle took off from the *Hornet* (top and above), hitting Tokyo and other Japanese cities. Less than a month later, at the Battle of the Coral Sea, the Americans lost the *Lexington* (below) but won a key strategic victory.

Chapter Two
The Forces Gather

June 2–3, 1942

A HALF HOUR BEFORE DAWN ON JUNE 2, 1942, THE SHIP'S company of U.S.S. *Yorktown* mustered to general quarters just as it had on each of its previous days at sea since joining the war in the Pacific. With the coming of first light, the huge aircraft carrier—one of the most powerful ships in the United States Navy—turned into the wind and launched scout planes to scour the seascape ahead of its course and on both flanks for any sign of the enemy. Then, once the dawn hour of danger had passed, the men stood down from their battle stations. All but those on watch duty headed to their respective messes for breakfast, a considerably better meal than had been seen on board in quite a while. On May 30, the *Yorktown* had sortied from Pearl Harbor with its first load of fresh provisions in months. Until its return to Oahu on May 27, the ship had been almost continuously at sea for 101 days.

Only one month before, at the Battle of the Coral Sea, the *Yorktown* had been hit by a 550-pound (250 kg) bomb that had penetrated nearly down to the armored deck and exploded in an aviation storeroom above the engineering spaces. It had killed or severely wounded 66 men and had left a huge hollow inside the hull. Everyone on board, from Capt. Elliott Buckmaster on down, had expected repairs to the damage to take a few weeks, but the

Dauntless dive-bombers fly in formation high above the American fleet.

work crews at Pearl Harbor had been ordered to fix the ship in only three days. Now here they were heading back out to sea and into battle. Just how big the battle would be, no one knew. But there was a Japanese fleet aimed at Midway, and it was their job to stop it.

Spirits were high despite the ridiculously short shore leave at Pearl. The long voyage in the South Pacific and the *Yorktown*'s fine performance at the Coral Sea had welded the ship's company into a close-knit community. Captain Buckmaster, at times an austere and distant figure, had won the hearts of his men by his expert conning, or directing the steering, of the ship during the Japanese attack. At Pearl he had assured all hands that when the coming battle was over, there would be a long layover at the Puget Sound Navy Yard in Bremerton, Washington, with a major furlough stateside for the crew. This meant there would be time to see parents, siblings, girl-friends, and wives. As Lt. Comdr. Clarence "Jug" Ray, the *Yorktown*'s communications officer, would later remember, "That announcement restored morale 100 percent."

(Above) The *Yorktown* enters Pearl Harbor in February 1942. Her crew would be at sea for the next three months, until just before Midway. (Below) Bill Surgi, far right, works on a fighter's landing wheel in a scene captured by the famed photographer Edward Steichen.

Aviation Machinist's Mate 3rd Class William Surgi shared the general mood of optimism, but for him it was tinged with a few dark thoughts. He had had a close shave at the Battle of the Coral Sea when shrapnel from the bomb blast killed the man standing next to him. Now he couldn't help wondering if the *Yorktown*—including the flight crews—was truly ready for combat. Especially VF-3, or Fighting Three, the fighter squadron recently arrived on board and leavened with veterans from Surgi's VF-42. The squadron's boss, Lt. Comdr. John S. "Jimmy" Thach, was already known as one of the most savvy fighter pilots in the fleet. But the band of greenhorns he led was quite another matter. Surgi would never forget what happened when the planes of Fighting Three landed on the carrier's flight deck as it headed northwest from Oahu after leaving Pearl Harbor. Thach's landing had been picture perfect; so had that of his seasoned executive officer, Lt. Comdr. Donald Lovelace. But the man who came in third landed badly, leaping the barrier and crashing into Lovelace's brand-new

Wildcat as it taxied forward. The airplane's propeller had chopped up Lovelace's cockpit and the man in it. There was a replacement for the aircraft, but not for Lovelace himself, who had flown it with such skill and confidence.

Presumably such thoughts crossed the minds of many of the 2,300 men on the *Yorktown* as she sped northwestward, but none had as much to think about as Rear Adm. Frank Jack Fletcher, whose decisions would direct the Americans when and if the Japanese turned up. Fletcher's ship was not in the fighting trim he would have liked.

Her insides were shored up with wooden supports, and her flight crews had been cobbled together from just about every available source, including refugees from the carrier *Saratoga*, torpedoed by a Japanese submarine the previous January and seriously damaged. His escort would be perilously thin—only two heavy cruisers and five destroyers—in the event of a powerful air attack. Half of his fliers had never seen combat before.

The 57-year-old admiral was also mentally tired and physically exhausted. When he had met with Adm. Chester Nimitz, commander in chief of the Pacific Fleet, during the *Yorktown*'s brief layover in Hawaii, observers noted that his hands shook

For Rear Adm. Frank Jack Fletcher and his crew, there would be no time to rest during their three days at Pearl Harbor.

with a slight palsy and his manner seemed untypically languorous. Fletcher badly needed a rest. Instead he was facing the biggest test of his naval career.

At 1600 hours, the *Yorktown* arrived at the appointed rendezvous: 32° north, 173° west. There she was met by two other carriers, the *Enterprise* and the *Hornet*. Together these three ships formed the striking heart of a sizable American force, the greatest yet assembled in the first year of the war in the Pacific: 3 aircraft carriers, 8 heavy cruisers, 1 light cruiser, and 15 destroyers. Nevertheless, the Americans made a puny showing next to what the Japanese could throw at them if they chose: at least 4 fast carriers and 4 light carriers, plus 11 battleships, including the *Yamato*, the largest and most powerful warship yet built.

The Japanese had divided their forces into four fleets. One fleet operated far to the north, its target the Aleutian Islands; one carried the troops for the invasion; another force, to the rear, was centered by Yamamoto's flagship. And in the vanguard was Vice Adm. Chuichi Nagumo's striking force, the *kido butai*, as it was known in Japanese, with its four big carriers.

Admiral Nimitz knew what sort of gamble he was taking. If he lost his three aircraft carriers, or flattops, and their planes there was nothing to take their place. No wonder he had nicknamed the rendezvous "Point Luck." Nimitz understood that luck, as well as skill, would be needed for any hope of victory in the battle to come.

Nimitz's instructions to Fletcher and to Fletcher's second in command, Rear Adm. Raymond Spruance, who flew his flag from the *Yorktown*'s sister the *Enterprise*, epitomized his style of command. They were straightforward and devoid of bombast: "In carrying out the task assigned . . . you will be governed by the principle of calculated risk, which you shall interpret to mean avoidance of exposure of your force to attack by superior enemy forces without good prospect of inflicting, as a result of such exposure, greater damage on the enemy." This mission was easy in theory but devilishly difficult in practice.

Breaking the Code

A modern personal computer could break Japan's World War II naval code in a matter of minutes. In the spring of 1942, however, it took cryptanalysts in Australia, Washington, D.C., and Hawaii untold hours of intense effort to achieve the breakthrough that made an American victory at Midway possible. The Japanese naval code, known as JN 25, consisted of approximately 45,000 five-digit numbers, each number representing a word or a phrase. Breaking this code, which was modified regularly, meant divining the meanings of enough of these numbers that a whole message could be decrypted by extrapolating the missing parts. According to one of the leading codebreakers involved, it was like putting together a jigsaw puzzle with most of its pieces always missing.

Leading the codebreaking effort was Station Hypo, the code name for the combat intelligence unit at Pearl Harbor under Comdr. Joseph Rochefort. In the dank, air-conditioned basement where the intelligence teams worked, Rochefort padded around in bedroom slippers with a bathrobe thrown over his seldom-pressed uniform. Rochefort and his staff could work virtually nonstop, and often went for days on a few hours' sleep.

By May 8, Rochefort knew that a major enemy operation, whose objective was sometimes called AF, was in the offing and that it would take place somewhere in the Central Pacific. Several days later, he was sure the target was Midway. His superiors in Washington weren't convinced, so he and his team devised a test that would flush out the location of AF.

The radio station on Midway dispatched an uncoded message falsely reporting that the water distillation plant on the island had broken down, causing a severe water shortage. Within 48 hours, Station Hypo decrypted a Japanese radio transmission alerting commanders that AF was short of water. And by May 27, when the Japanese finally got around to modifying the current version of JN 25, Rochefort had built up such a detailed picture of their plans that Lt. Comdr. Edwin Layton, Admiral Nimitz's intelligence officer, was able to predict almost precisely when and where the enemy striking force would appear.

(Above) Some of Rochefort's crew in their basement lair. Many of these sailors were bandsmen from the battleship *California,* damaged at Pearl Harbor. Rochefort thought their musical skills might make them adept codebreakers. (Above right) Comdr. Joseph Rochefort, the officer in charge of Station Hypo, as he looked a decade earlier, during language studies in Japan.

Now that their ships were in sight of one another, the two admirals could communicate using signal lamps, eliminating any chance of alerting the Japanese to their presence. In the event that weather made this impossible, they could resort to TBS radio—a low-frequency radio that permitted talk between ships—one of the Americans' clear technological advantages over their Japanese adversaries, who risked breaking radio silence with every voice communication. TBS permitted close-range radio contact that could not be detected by enemy listening.

In accordance with instructions from Admiral Nimitz, who had carefully directed the disposition of all the American forces that would face the Japanese, Fletcher now divided his ships into two separate tactical units. While retaining overall command, he ordered Spruance with his two carriers to operate independently at a distance of ten miles from him. This would allow the carriers to adapt to changing circumstances as the fight developed and would deny the enemy a single concentrated target for attack.

When Vice Adm. William "Bull" Halsey (right) came down with a bad bout of dermatitis just before Midway, he nominated Rear Adm. Raymond Spruance (left) to assume command of Task Force 16 (*Enterprise* and *Hornet*), even though Spruance was not a naval aviator and had never commanded a carrier.

Bill Surgi has no clear memory of the *Yorktown*'s afternoon rendezvous with the two other carriers. Too many years have passed and too many more vivid events soon crowded out this one. As an enlisted man, he knew nothing of the tactical talk between admirals that might have etched it in his mind. His job was to look after his "Airedales"—the enlisted man's nickname for the flying elite—and to man his battle station when required. When he wasn't on duty, he could come topside for a breath of air. That afternoon, as usual, a lone seabird trailed in the ship's wake, hoping to scavenge what these human seafarers discarded. Surgi watched it ride the air currents with what seemed like amazing ease.

Someone had told him that the bird was an albatross, but at the time, he was ignorant of the albatross's ominous reputation. According to superstition, each albatross carries the soul of a drowned sailor that brings with it portents of death. Nor did Surgi know that this particular species, the Laysan albatross, whose wingspan typically reaches ten feet, breeds in great numbers on the tiny atoll known as Midway.

DURING THE MORNING OF JUNE 3, A THICK, SHELTERING FOG SHROUDED THE *KIDO BUTAI* UNDER Vice Admiral Nagumo as it steamed relentlessly toward Midway. Consisting of two fast battleships, two heavy cruisers (each capable of launching five floatplane scouts) one light cruiser, and 12 destroyers, as well as its four flattops, this was, except for the absence of two carriers damaged at the Coral Sea, essentially the same force under the same commander that had launched the surprise attack on Pearl Harbor six months before. If, as Nagumo believed, his fleet was as yet undetected, the fog virtually ensured him the advantage of surprise. Unfortunately, however, it prevented his ships, which were under strict radio silence, from communicating by means of visual signals.

As Nagumo's task force approached a scheduled 1030 course change, the admiral and his staff stood on the starboard side of the *Akagi*'s bridge "staring silently at the impenetrable curtain surrounding the ship," each face "tense with anxiety." The description belongs to Comdr. Mitsuo Fuchida, senior strike leader of the First Air Fleet, who, except for the recent emergency removal of his appendix, would have been flying in the Midway operation. The fog was too heavy to coordinate the scheduled course change without breaking radio silence. Use the radio and Nagumo risked revealing his presence to the enemy.

Nagumo's anxiety stemmed from more than the question of whether to break his precious radio silence. The fog had become a metaphor for his ignorance of the opposition he would face. Did an American fleet await him, or would he find Midway unattended and weakly defended? If headquarters knew anything, he hadn't heard it. Admiral Yamamoto and his staff exercised overall command of the Midway operation from Japan's huge new battleship, *Yamato*, positioned several hundred miles to Nagumo's rear. So obsessed was Yamamoto's staff with maintaining radio silence that they had failed to inform Nagumo of the sharp increase in radio traffic around Hawaii or the various sightings of American submarines and scout planes—all evidence that his arrival was expected.

Vice Adm. Chuichi Nagumo had led the First Mobile Force to victory after victory in the first six months of the war, but some of his subordinates worried that he was out of his depth when it came to carrier-to-carrier warfare.

Lacking any intelligence of the enemy's strength or disposition, Nagumo faced a tactical conundrum. He had been handed two competing missions. Mission one: bomb Midway. Mission two: destroy any American force that challenged him. Which job came first depended on the presence or absence in the vicinity of Midway of an enemy fleet that included aircraft carriers. A Japanese proverb summed up Nagumo's dilemma precisely: "He who pursues two hares catches neither."

As the time for the course change drew near, Nagumo and his advisers debated their course of action. Comdr. Tamotsu Oishi pointed out that while their priority was to destroy the American carriers, their first order of business was the air attack on Midway scheduled for the following morning. "But where is the enemy fleet?" plaintively asked the admiral. Finally they decided: Make the course change as planned,

Midway Gamblers

The opposing strategists, Adm. Isoroku Yamamoto (right) and Adm. Chester Nimitz (left), each took an enormous gamble at Midway. Nimitz committed most of his fleet, including his three aircraft carriers, hoping he could deliver a serious setback to the Japanese. Yamamoto banked on an elaborate plan (map bottom) involving five main forces and numerous subdivisions.

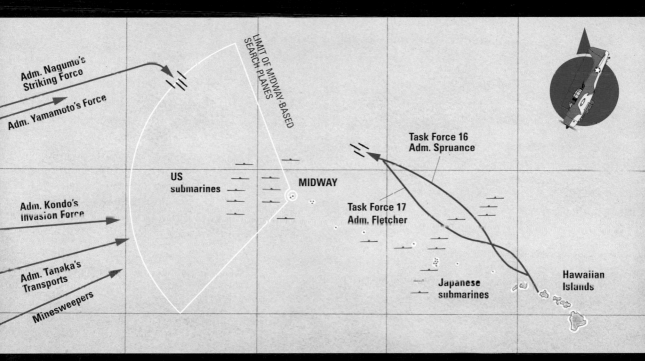

Adm. Nagumo's Striking Force

Adm. Yamamoto's Force

LIMIT OF MIDWAY-BASED SEARCH PLANES

US submarines

MIDWAY

Task Force 16 Adm. Spruance

Task Force 17 Adm. Fletcher

Adm. Kondo's Invasion Force

Adm. Tanaka's Transports

Minesweepers

Japanese submarines

Hawaiian Islands

Isoroku Yamamoto (above right) and Chester Nimitz (above left) stood above their contemporaries in terms of strategic vision. Both would risk almost everything if the situation warranted it.

ALEUTIAN FORCES

Aleutian Islands

MIDWAY FORCES

Midway Island

MIDWAY FORCES

Hawaiian Islands

On June 3 (map above), while Admiral Nagumo's *kido butai* (strike force) headed for Midway from the northwest and a powerful invasion force under Vice Adm. Nobutake Kondo steamed toward it from the southwest, a third fleet launched an air raid on the American base at Dutch Harbor, Alaska. The Japanese planned to bomb Midway on June 4, followed by a battleship bombardment on June 5. Kondo's force would occupy the island on June 6. Using Midway as an air base, Nagumo could handily defeat any counterattacking American fleet.

As the historian Samuel Eliot Morison would later write, "The vital defect in this sort of plan," which hinged on perfect timing and taking the enemy by surprise, "is that it depends on the enemy doing exactly what is expected." Fortunately for the Americans, Admiral Nimitz was a man capable of confounding expectations.

conveying the order by means of a low-frequency radio transmission that had a reasonable chance of avoiding detection. They would proceed on the assumption that there was no enemy fleet to worry about until it was proved otherwise.

Among the mighty assemblage of men and hardware that made up the Japanese striking force were two young airmen aboard the carrier *Kaga*. They, like many of their comrades, had faced the Americans before. Both Yuji Akamatsu, who had just celebrated his 22nd birthday, and Haruo Yoshino, who would turn 22 in three weeks, had flown in torpedo bombers in the victorious surprise attack on Pearl Harbor. Despite the glorious result, their squadron had lost five planes, and they had lost 15 friends, teaching them that even victory comes with a high cost. This time Yoshino would be flying reconnaissance—that is, if the fog ever lifted—while Akamatsu would be on antisubmarine patrol.

As Akamatsu would recall many years later, spirits were high despite the doubts lurking beneath the aura of invincibility then surrounding the Imperial Japanese Navy. Training for the Midway mission had been much less rigorous than the preparation for the Pearl Harbor attack. Six months of hard fighting had taken their toll, too. Along with the veterans on board were many raw recruits with no battle experience. And this time, surely, the Americans would not be caught napping. Nor could the young airman help wondering at the wisdom of occupying a tiny atoll so far from Japan's sources of supply or whether his small country could hold on to an empire that encompassed more than half of the Pacific Ocean.

Akamatsu found it odd that even though the Japanese armada was thousands of kilometers from home, the clocks on board were still set to Tokyo time. As a result, shipboard routines were badly out of sync with the evidence of one's senses: Breakfast took place around midday and dinner in mid-evening. It made for "a strange sort of life," he remembered. Such stubborn adherence to fixed patterns typified the rigidity of the whole Japanese war machine. But why change a winning way? In the six months since the attack on Pearl Harbor, the navy of the emperor had known almost nothing but victory.

All through the afternoon and into the night of June 3, the great fleet plowed blindly forward, believing that it still held the advantage of surprise, unsure whether any enemy aircraft carriers were close enough to come to Midway's aid, yet fundamentally unquestioning of its superiority over any force the Americans might throw in its way. But not everyone thought this way. From his convalescent bed in the *Akagi's* sick bay, Mitsuo Fuchida felt an ominous ache unconnected to his recent surgery. "The storm of battle was about to break," he later wrote, "and for the first time in six months, Fate did not seem to be smiling upon us. No change, however, was made in the operational plan. All forces plunged onward through the boundless fog like stagecoach horses driven blindly forward by a cracking whip."

(Opposite) Haruo Yoshino, at far left, and Yuji Akamatsu in their flight gear. Both had flown in the attack on Pearl Harbor. (Right) Harry Ferrier poses with the twin machine guns of an American carrier plane. For him and his comrades, Midway would be their first battle.

THE NIGHT OF JUNE 3–4, 1942, PASSED IN TENSE AND FITFUL SLEEP FOR THE THOUSANDS OF men crowded into tents and dugouts on Midway's Sand and Eastern Islands, among them 18 fliers from the *Hornet's* Torpedo Squadron Eight, who had arrived from Hawaii just three days before in six brand-spanking-new Grumman TBF-1 torpedo bombers, also known as Avengers. The airplanes were among a total of 19 new planes that had reached Hawaii one day too late to join the rest of their squadron already based aboard the *Hornet*. Instead, in by far the longest flight of their infant careers, the inexperienced pilots had flown to Midway.

When the Torpedo Eight detachment had come in to land, 18-year-old radioman Harry Ferrier thought that Eastern Island, which held the airstrip, looked like a "big sandbar covered with airplanes," so solid was the tiny island with aircraft parked wingtip to wingtip. The previous few weeks had witnessed a remarkable buildup of American forces, Navy, Army, and Marine. Every plane that could fit on the two tiny islands now sat on Midway. But this was hardly an air force to strike fear into Admiral Nagumo's heart: the planes either verged on obsolete or, in the *(continued on page 42)*

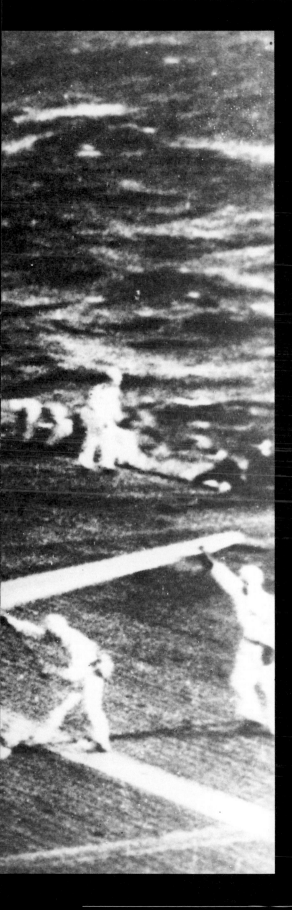

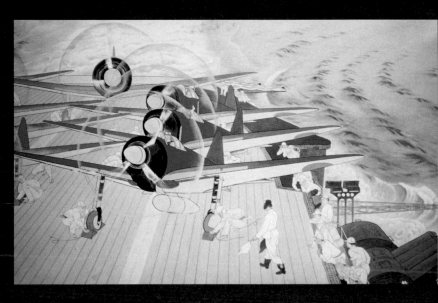

The Carrier Striking Force

Admiral Nagumo's reservations about the Midway operation included concerns about the preparedness of his crews, many of whom were untested in battle. All but one of his carriers had been in dry dock during training exercises in the Inland Sea, and the rehearsal had not been as thorough as the one that had preceded Pearl Harbor. Nonetheless, the *kido butai* represented Japan's elite naval striking force, with seasoned commanders and veteran fliers at its core. In fact, the greatest fault with the Nagumo force was its overconfidence.

(Opposite) An action shot of Strike Force Zeros preparing to take off for Pearl Harbor contrasts with (top and above) these graceful, classically styled renderings of the same planes aboard a Japanese carrier.

(continued from page 39) case of the squadron of high-altitude army B-17 bombers, would prove sadly ineffective as anti-ship weapons. Tragically lacking was anything like the necessary number of fighter aircraft to escort the bombers and torpedo planes soon to be sent against the Japanese fleet. Few of the pilots and crew who would be flying them had any notion of what they were getting into.

Harry Ferrier's 25-year-old pilot, Ens. Albert K. Earnest, surely breathed at least one small sigh of relief when their airplane touched down. He had only earned his wings in November 1941. The flight from Oahu was his first out of sight of land. In

fact not one man among them had previously faced combat.

Ferrier's youthfulness was not unusual. In the dying days of the Great Depression, with war looming, many thousands of young Americans had signed up for armed service. Ferrier had an extra reason for wanting to leave home. He and his stepfather, an abusive alcoholic, didn't get along. Harry's mother helped him fake his birth certificate so that he could enlist a year below the legal age on January 28, 1941, just five days after his 16th birthday. He had wanted to see the world. Now he was getting his wish: You couldn't get much farther from his home in New England than Midway.

SLEEP CAME UNEASILY, IF AT ALL, TO THE COMMANDING ADMIRALS ON BOTH SIDES. EVEN Raymond Spruance, noted for his unflappability under the most trying circumstances, a man who reportedly never missed his night's rest, must have sat up late. He was facing the biggest test of his career and he knew it. As for Admiral Fletcher, it would take more than one night's sleep to relieve his bone-deep fatigue. He had already followed one order—to divide his forces—for which he would be roundly criticized if the outcome went against him. His next decisions would have to be taken in the heat of battle with no time for reflection. As he would later comment, "After a battle is over, people talk a lot about how the decisions were methodically made, but actually there's a hell of a lot of groping around."

Fletcher's counterpart, Admiral Nagumo, still had no idea that his approach was expected or that a powerful American fleet lay in wait. In fact one prong of the complex Japanese advance had already been discovered. The previous morning (June 3), a Catalina flying boat from Midway had spotted the invasion force under the command of Adm. Kondo steaming toward Midway from the west. By nightfall Midway had launched one high-level bombing attack on this fleet but had scored no hits. Thus Admiral Yamamoto knew his invasion force had been found, but he still would not break radio silence to convey this invaluable information to Nagumo, the man who needed it the most.

(Opposite) Before the war, Midway had been a way station for Pan-Am flying boats en route to the Far East. The station would be badly damaged during the battle, but today its remains are one of the 63 structures dating from the battle that still stand on the atoll (above).

Nonetheless, a warrior of Nagumo's age and experience had to be prepared for anything. But some of those around him questioned his suitability for such a weighty command. Commander Fuchida, who had served as a junior destroyer officer under then-Captain Nagumo, was struck by the change in his beloved former commander now that he wore the gold braid of an admiral. To be sure, his assessment, made after the war, undoubtedly contains elements of self-justification and the natural impatience of a younger man, with fewer responsibilities than an older one, who must worry about the fate of a whole fleet. Still, his memories give the impression of a commander out of his depth. "I began to feel dissatisfied with his apparent conservatism and passiveness," Fuchida wrote. "Personally he was as warm-hearted as ever, but his once-vigorous fighting spirit seemed to be gone, and with it his stature as an outstanding naval leader. Instead he seemed rather average, and I was suddenly aware of his increased age."

Before the Battle of Midway, no smart gambler would have placed a heavy bet on either side. The Japanese, with their superior fleet, more experienced air crews, far more effective torpedoes, and faster and more agile fighter aircraft, were clearly ahead on points when simply stacking one fleet against the other. On the other hand, the Americans retained the priceless element of surprise as well as at least two other important tactical advantages: shorter lines of supply and radar. Midway may lie roughly halfway between Japan and North America, but in 1942 it lay far closer to

the major American naval base at Pearl Harbor than to a major Japanese one. The Japanese fleet train—the slowly moving oilers and repair ships—had to trudge hundreds of additional miles to supply their fleet.

Radar's importance at this stage of the Pacific war is more difficult to measure. The Americans had it on Midway and on almost all of their ships; the Japanese approaching Midway had none. But the Japanese were extremely skilled at reconnaissance and aerial navigation. And if it came to a night engagement, their superior training clearly offset radar at this stage of its development.

If one factor above all others favored the Americans, it was psychological: The U.S. commanders had a realistic assessment of the difficulties ahead and of the skill of their enemy; the Japanese did not. After their virtually uninterrupted string of victories, the Japanese had succumbed to a terminal case of overconfidence—what Fuchida and others would later call "victory disease." They considered the Americans inferior in every way, lacking in skill and in fighting spirit. When dawn broke over the Pacific at 0437 on June 4, and over two great fleets and one tiny atoll crowded with men, ordnance, munitions, and flying machines, the Americans' readiness for battle would be the biggest surprise of all.

Shortly after 0900 on June 3, a Catalina flying boat piloted by Ens. Jack Reid spotted Admiral Kondo's occupation force, which had arrived ahead of schedule within scouting range of Midway.

AMONG THOSE WHO WOULD LIVE TO DESCRIBE TO THEIR CHILDREN AND GRANDCHILDREN THE part they played were the four who would revisit the field of battle 56 years later. At dawn, Haruo Yoshino had already taken off from the *Kaga* on the first reconnaissance flight of the day. Yuji Akamatsu was patrolling for submarines in advance of the Japanese fleet, which had already launched its attacking force against Midway. On Midway, Harry Ferrier and the other 17 members of the Torpedo Eight detachment started their engines at first light, watched eagerly for the signal to take off, then were ordered to stand down. They waited, anxious to get into the air and see some action at last. Aboard the *Yorktown*, Bill Surgi stopped at his locker before heading for his battle station. He took a moment to handle his father's Bluejacket's Manual from World War I, when the old man had commanded a company of recruits at the Great Lakes Naval Training Station in Michigan. He couldn't help thinking how much his father would have liked to be a part of the coming action. Then he headed topside to greet the dawning of the day that would see the greatest naval battle since Jutland.

A Happy Ship

To a man, former members of the *Yorktown*'s crew describe her as a happy ship, which explains the strong affection many still feel toward her.

The crew's sense of community grew out of shared hardship: convoy duty in the storm-wracked North Atlantic before America was officially at war; the lengthy stint away from base in the southern Pacific in the spring of 1942, a record unbroken by any U.S. carrier until Operation Desert Storm during the 1991 Gulf War.

It helped to have officers who were respected. Captain Buckmaster's superb ship handling during the Battle of the Coral Sea made him a hero: as he took his seat at the first movie night following the battle, he was given a standing ovation by the crew. But more than any other officer, Comdr. Dixie Kiefer, the ship's executive officer, was responsible for the *Yorktown*'s high morale at the time of Midway. Vane Bennett, then a warrant officer, remembers that the first time Kiefer walked into the ward room he had a cribbage board under

The paintings (here and over) by the American war artist William Draper depict typical scenes of aircraft carrier life: Pilots play cards in their ready room (opposite) and crewmen sort antiaircraft shells on the flight deck (above). (Top) The crest of U.S.S. *Yorktown*.

Mechanics (above) swarm over torpedo bombers in preparation for the next mission. (Below left) A pilot and mechanic on *Yorktown*'s flight deck work on an engine. Signalmen flash a Morse message by lamp (below center) from the carrier's signal bridge, located just above the pilothouse. The *Yorktown*'s popular executive officer, Dixie Kiefer (in lifejacket, below right), watches air traffic. (Opposite page) The chow got worse as a voyage lengthened (top), but the ship's swing band, aided by the jitterbugging prowess of Sid Flum and Pete Montalvo (center), helped maintain morale. Behind them is a mural showing the ship's voyages. (Bottom) Sailors and marines line the decks during *Yorktown*'s commissioning in 1937. When completed, she and her sisters, the *Enterprise* and the *Hornet*, were among the most powerful ships in the United States Navy.

his arm and asked, "Anyone
or a game?"

Such behavior goes a long
way in the feudal world of a naval
ship, where the captain is king,
he officers are privileged barons,
and the enlisted men little more
han serfs. (The black mess
stewards who waited on the
officers completed the picture of
social stratification.) There were
so many people on this huge ship
that an enlisted man rarely knew
anyone beyond his division. He
bunked with other members of his
division and he ate with them.
And unless his job required him
to roam outside his particular
precinct, it was all he knew.

The flying elite were a
race apart, on board the ship but
not truly of it. Whenever home
port neared, they flew their
planes ashore and didn't return
until the ship headed back out to
sea. Unlike the regular crew,
naval aviators regularly moved
between ships.

All elements of *Yorktown*
society came together on the
hangar deck beside the No. 2
elevator, an open space that
functioned as a kind of
community center. It was here
that Chaplain Frank Hamilton
conducted Sunday services,
where movies were shown to the
assembled crew, and where the
ship's big band rehearsed and
performed. On one occasion, a
group of the men put on a variety
show using the elevator platform,
raised a few feet above deck level,
as their stage.

As John Miller, one of the
surviving "plank owners"
members of the commissioning
crew) recalled, "That ship was
something special."

Chapter Three
Primary Target

Tuesday, May 5, 1998

I LIKE WANDERING THROUGH A SHIP AT NIGHT. EVEN THOUGH I KNOW THE *LANEY* WELL and have sailed on board her several times, she seems bigger and even a little mysterious when most of the people on board are safely tucked in their bunks. The shipboard sounds that fade into the background during the day move forward: the vibration of the engine, the sound of the wind, the pounding of water against the metal hull. And the pervasive shipboard smell of diesel fumes mixed with engine oil seems more pungent in the wee hours.

I didn't bother to get fully dressed, just threw on jogging sweats, then tiptoed out of my cabin so as not to disturb my cabin mate, Bruce Appelgate. Once in the corridor, I became more aware of the pounding on the ship's hull, which meant we were tracking into the wind and waves. The gangway ladder—stairs are always ladders on a ship—is narrow enough that I can grasp both rails, chilly metal even on a tropical night, and use them to lighten my feet so that I can almost glide down the two flights, except for a brief pause at the landing, in one seamless motion. It's something I've been doing since I was a kid.

At the foot of the ladder, I was on the main deck. If I took two paces forward and turned right, I'd be in the wet lab. Instead, I continued straight ahead, walking directly into the War Room. I stared briefly at the chart on the light table. No inspiration there. Then I walked through the door into the wet lab. Karen and Nathan were glued to their computer screens, hands dancing over keys while New Age music played softly in the background. Karen's station made me think of a nest or a burrow; she'd added several personal touches to make it homey—above all a picture of her ten-year-old son Max taped to the top of her computer monitor. As usual, she's wearing her fluffy, bright purple slippers, jeans, and an aloha shirt. She's definitely a night owl.

In an early-morning recovery, our ATV is hauled aboard the *Laney Chouest*.

They didn't even know I was there until I spoke. I asked Karen if she could spare a minute. She followed me back into the War Room. I asked her whether any of the targets we had highlighted looked promising to her.

"I'd say our two primary targets are too big," she told me. "And they look too much like backscatter from the edges of geologic features."

"Where does that leave us?"

"Well," she continued, "I've been looking at another feature that I kind of like. I have a gut feeling about it. When it caught my eye, I just sensed that this was it."

Karen was talking a language I know and love, where science meets intuition. It's the language I live and breathe.

"Go for it," I told her.

She promised to examine the target from every angle and let me know in the morning if it panned out. Feeling better than I had all day, I headed off to bed.

Wednesday, May 6

WHEN I WENT DOWN TO THE WAR ROOM BEFORE BREAKFAST THIS MORNING, KAREN Sender was waiting for me. Dave Mindell, who had been up all night keeping an eye on things, looked haggard, but there was no way he was going to bed if Karen had something interesting to say.

"Okay, Karen," I began. "Make my day."

"Well, all I can say for sure is that my target meets all your criteria. And I believe it's the only target in the data that adds up to a possible *Yorktown*."

"What makes you so sure?"

"Look at the surveys," she told me.

We walked over to the chart table. Karen pointed to the target she had identified—a tiny grain of rice that looked like quite a few others. Then she flipped up the top layer to reveal a previous run that had passed within range of the same spot. The target seemed to have shifted, but it was the same size and shape. I looked at her.

"I think these two are the same target," she said. "We can blame the offset on that sync error between the ship's clock and the sonar clock. Remember, we corrected it after we ran that line."

Underneath that sonar run was yet another sheet that showed an identically shaped target. Its position was much closer to the first.

I was beginning to feel better. If Karen was right in her calculations and this was a single target, we had satisfied our first and most important criterion: It looked the same from every angle.

"Now look at the first two east–west lines we ran," she added.

Both of those lines happened to run right above the target, which put it in *MR-1*'s blind spot but perfectly placed for a reading from its depth sounder.

Once the ATV is in the water, the twilight world of the control van becomes our nerve center. Monitors show the results of the sonar search and anything picked up by underwater cameras while the navy pilot uses a joystick to maneuver the vehicle three miles down.

"I went back over the depth data ping by ping," Karen continued. "The depth change appears to be appropriate for an aircraft carrier."

"How much?"

"Thirteen meters."

The *Yorktown* was about 90 feet, or 27.5 meters, high from keel to flight deck. After she'd fallen three miles, it made sense for her to be buried halfway in the mud. (I remembered the *Titanic*'s half-buried bow.)

"What do you think, Dave?" I asked.

"Looks awfully good," Dave replied. "Right smack in the middle of the highest probability area and located in a spot that's consistent with our destroyer fixes and the way we assume the ship drifted in the current."

As he so often does, Dave said what I was thinking. All of us were getting more and more excited as we went over the data again.

Word quickly spread that we had found something. Soon the War Room was standing room only as everyone craned to get a look at our now-favorite target. Peter Schnall and his crew arrived to film me as I recapitulated the analysis that led us to believe we had found the ship. Soon my words were bolstered with enlarged images of the target produced by the *MR-1* team. By now the blip on the paper was beginning to look like a ship. I could almost imagine it. It was uncanny.

I began sounding more confident than I felt. To anyone who asked, I'd announce: "That's it. That's the *Yorktown*. I'm sure we've got it." But I knew better. There are just too many variables in this business. In this case these included the ATV, which was sitting on the stern with its tether cut in half while its Navy nursemaids worked to repair the shorted connection.

But tonight as I hit the rack, I'm feeling better than I have since the expedition began. Karen's target sure seems like the *Yorktown*. I can almost taste it.

Thursday, May 7

TODAY'S EVENTS ARE ALMOST TOO PAINFUL TO WRITE ABOUT, but maybe getting them down on paper will help. This morning I awoke after my best sleep of the expedition so far, filled with a mixture of great anticipation and self-doubt. Is it really the *Yorktown* down there?

Every launch of the ATV (above) seemed to bring new technical problems. A short circuit meant cutting the ATV's tether and sorting through fistfuls of insulation (below). (Opposite) A naval technician adjusts the extra lights we added to the ATV.

After breakfast I put on my *Yorktown* hat—a baseball cap with a *Yorktown* Association insignia on it that one of the survivors sent me—and began to study the model of the ship that Chuck Haberlein brought with him. I wondered what shape the wreck would be in. We know from all the eyewitnesses that it left the surface in one piece, but it had also borne a lot of punishment: three bomb hits and some near misses astern, two airplane-launched torpedoes, and, the *coup de grâce*, two powerful submarine-launched torpedoes. If it had broken, where might the break have been? Perhaps where the structure had been weakened by the bomb hit during the earlier Battle of the Coral Sea.

Coral Sea. I suddenly realized that today—May 7—was the 56th anniversary of that battle, the first aircraft carrier battle in naval history, the first time two fleets engaged without surface ships on either side actually seeing each other. Coral Sea. The battle that set the stage for Midway. I was sure that Bill Surgi was marking the day in some way. Not only had he been on the *Yorktown* during the battle, he had also helped found the Battle of the Coral Sea Association. I wondered if Admiral Fletcher had become a member. Despite losing one carrier (the *Lexington*) and almost losing another (the *Yorktown*), he had scored an important strategic victory—turning back the Japanese advance on Port Moresby.

At the time, the Battle of the Coral Sea looked like at best a draw—the Japanese judged it a narrow victory—but Nimitz had no hesitation in sending Fletcher right back into the lion's den. In a message to his boss in Washington, Adm. Ernest J. King, who had been agitating for Fletcher's removal, Nimitz wrote, "Fletcher did a fine

job and exercised superior judgement in his recent cruise to the Coral Sea. He is an excellent, seagoing, fighting naval officer."

I was starting to get lost in my 1942 reverie when Dave Mindell came into the lab to inform me that the reterminated cable on the ATV had failed to pass its tests and that another day might be needed to fix it. So much for putting on my game face.

In the end it took only five hours to find and fix the problem—but it was another five precious hours wasted. We have our search sonar for only two weeks. We can't afford to waste much more time here before heading out to look for the Japanese carriers.

At 1600, the ATV finally hit the water, which meant another three hours of waiting while it made its slow descent. I ate dinner without even noticing the food. Talked with Tom Allen, a NATIONAL GEOGRAPHIC writer on the expedition. The waiting drove me crazy, but I stayed away from the control van until I received word that we were approaching the bottom.

The ATV control van sits on the *Laney*'s raised afterdeck, separated from the forward superstructure by a stretch of wave-washed deck. It's become a game to get across that stretch without getting your feet wet—and that's with rubber boots on. The trick is to time your dash to coincide with the roll of the ship. I've noticed that even the four old navy vets are getting pretty good at this. But it's always an adventure.

The van itself, which sits on the starboard side of the afterdeck, is about half the size of the control areas I'm accustomed to and twice as crowded. Space is at such a premium, in fact, that Jay Minkin, the video technician I have brought along on the expedition, has had to set up his workstation in the entranceway, a space so narrow that he can't even sit down. To enter the van, you first have to squeeze past him. When all the Navy operatives are at their posts and the film team is in position, there's barely room to move. I've found that my best vantage point is an upturned trash can, cushioned by a pillow, just behind the ATV's pilot and co-pilot. That way I can see the screens over their shoulders.

When I arrived no one was talking. The atmosphere was tight with expectation. At moments like this one, I always feel the accumulated tension, the weight of all the preparation and all the hopes riding on an expedition. A lot of people are expecting us to find the *Yorktown*. After all, Bob Ballard always finds his ship. That's what they think. But that's not always what happens.

When we reached 500 meters (1,640 feet) above bottom, Jay started the videotape rolling. Jay may be an expert video technician but he's a greenhorn when it comes to looking for shipwrecks. (He's more likely to be found working on the daytime soap opera *Another World* than where he is right now—midway between nowhere and nowhere.) Over the next few hours, I knew that if we found the ship, his mettle would be tested. Right behind me sat Chief Michael Swarm, in charge of the U.S. Navy team operating the ATV, watching as his team cautiously continued paying out cable. He and his colleagues knew that this was no routine

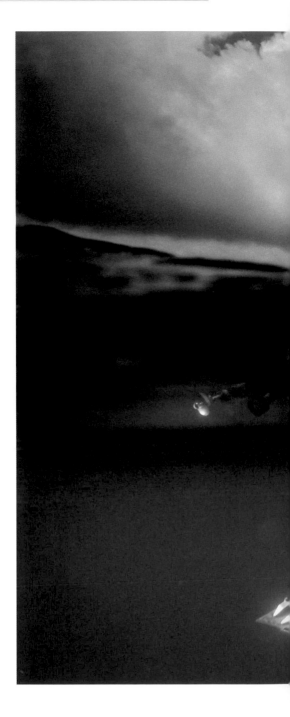

This dramatic split-frame shot by photographer David Doubilet shows the ATV beginning its descent with the *Laney Chouest* looming above.

mission: They were helping hunt for part of their own past, helping us revisit one of the great episodes in U.S. naval history.

At any moment we expected to see the muddy battlefield three miles below. Although I knew it made no difference, I stared at the blue video screen more intently, as if I could will a shipwreck to materialize out of the void.

"There's something funny here," muttered Jay.

Barely had he spoken than a milky cloud filled the video screen. Then the screen went black.

My first thought was that we had hit bottom. The ATV was operating at only about 75 percent owing to a number of technical problems, including ones I haven't even bothered to record. One system not online was the near-bottom altimeter. Now that we had reached an altitude of 500 meters above the bottom, we were relying on a camera trained on a mechanical depth gauge—a rough-and-ready rig, but it did the job. Now, without video, we were lost. My second thought was that we had wrecked the vehicle, maybe even lost it, which would put a finish to our expedition almost before it had started.

Chief Swarm suggested that we had better initiate recovery, the three-hour process of reeling the vehicle back in, but I was reluctant to give up just yet. I wanted a look at the *Yorktown*. My gut told me the ship was down there, if only our remote eyeball could see it. Finally I bowed to the inevitable. Flying blind was pointless.

I asked Chief Swarm to begin slowly bringing the vehicle back to the surface. Suddenly the navigation team on the bridge reported that, although the cable was coming back in, the vehicle's transponder, which emits a signal indicating the ATV's position, wasn't moving. Did this mean the ATV had somehow broken loose and was sitting on the bottom? If so, our expedition was definitely toast.

Out of the million possibilities, what had gone wrong this time? Jay Minkin reran that last few seconds of tape: The milky cloud sure looked like a cloud of sediment. But I just couldn't see how a crash landing would knock out all the systems or knock the vehicle free of its tether. The ATV was far too sturdy, the speed of lowering far too conservative, its cable far too strongly attached. It looked as if I would have to wait three hours to find out the truth.

There was no sense sitting in the van and feeling sorry for myself, so I wandered back to the War Room to consider the prospects of finding another video robot.

We were only about an hour into the recovery of the ATV when Jay came rushing in. One of the video cameras came back on.

"The ATV is still there!" he told me. "But wait till you see what it looks like."

When I reached the van, the pilots were panning the camera over the vehicle—which looked like someone had thrown a grenade at it. The depth gauge was intact but its needle had been knocked off. We could see broken instruments and twisted metal but no sign of the Benthos pressure spheres we'd had specially made to protect the batteries that power our expensive high-intensity lights. The evidence suggested a severe underwater implosion. Our only consolation was that the vehicle seemed to be in one piece. How soon we could get it working again was anyone's guess. I felt sick.

From a peak of anticipation, our mission had suddenly crashed like a torpedo bomber shot down by Japanese antiaircraft fire. My mood had crashed along with it. I didn't yet know how badly the ATV had been hurt, but one thing was clear: Without it our whole Midway expedition was in jeopardy. I didn't even want to think about making that phone call to National Geographic and our other sponsors explaining our failure, then heading home with nothing. A particularly frustrating possibility now loomed: we might locate one or more aircraft carriers, but not be able to prove it. Without our underwater eyes, any discovery was pure hypothesis.

But dealing with the unexpected is what I get paid for. I sometimes think that finding sunken ships is easier than keeping the technology from self-destructing. Back in the dry lab, I huddled with Dave Mindell over our charts. Unless the Navy could repair its vehicle overnight, we had to consider dropping our current plans and steaming over to look for the four lost Japanese carriers northwest of Midway. But I was reluctant to leave. I really wanted to have the *Yorktown* in the bag.

After the ATV disaster: When the glass pressure spheres imploded as the vehicle neared the bottom, their expensive contents were reduced to powdered rubble.

Dave went off to talk to Chief Swarm, then returned to tell me that it would take the Navy team several days to restore the ATV to even minimal operation. That settled it. I metaphorically dumped the whole expedition schedule overboard and told the *Laney*'s skipper, Capt. Vic Gisclair, to steam west. Captain Vic is used to my sudden changes of plan, having been with me on several previous expeditions, including our Jason Project to the Sea of Cortes and our exploration of Iron Bottom Sound at Guadalcanal.

My chief of operations, Cathy Offinger, one of the true veterans on board, was already on the phone to Benthos, trying to get replacements for the pressure spheres and lights. Meanwhile, Chuck Haberlein joined Dave and me as we pondered the search area we had laid out for the carriers *Kaga*, *Akagi*, and *Soryu*. Haberlein is the Navy historian who has analyzed the reported sinking positions of the Japanese ships as well as the American ones. Unfortunately Chuck hasn't had much to work with: The navigation logs were either lost during the battle or destroyed by the Japanese at the end of the war.

Finally, reluctantly, we called it a day and straggled off to our cabins.

As I write these words before turning in after this long and deeply dispiriting day, I'm conscious that the *Laney* is following a course that closely parallels the flight path of the carrier-launched bombers and torpedo planes that brought destruction to the Japanese fleet. Most of their pilots were too young and untested to be fearful. Most of those who are still around remember feeling only excited and confident. They had no inkling of the hell they were flying into.

Chapter Four
The Fourth of June

W E WERE QUITE AWARE THAT THE JAPANESE WERE WELL TRAINED and had a great deal of experience, something we did not have, but I don't think we dwelt on that," recalls Harry Ferrier. "We thought our airplane was so superior to the old model that our side had been flying that we were very excited. And if you have to go to war, you'd like to go in something that you have confidence in."

For the men who fought the Battle of Midway, the fourth of June, 1942, will always dawn with the same bold tropical sunrise that illuminated two powerful fleets racing toward their fateful meeting. On that day the four veterans who would return to Midway in spring 1998 were still more boys than men. The Battle of Midway would complete their passages into adulthood and would mark them for the rest of their lives.

Now in their seventies, the men each have vivid memories of the day that would change the course of the Pacific War.

"The majority of us were relatively green," Ferrier continues. "You could say pretty much the same thing about most of the pilots. None of us had ever flown in combat. But our enthusiasm overshadowed any doubt about whether we could fly when the time came. No, I don't think that ever occurred to me."

Yuji Akamatsu also remembers that morning: "The plan was to arrive at Midway at dawn, just as we had at Pearl Harbor. We still believed that the Americans had no idea we were coming. But we knew how dangerous the mission was and that many would not come back."

Haruo Yoshino was confident: "We were fresh from our latest victory, the attack on Ceylon, so our confidence and fighting spirit were high. We didn't worry about whether we would fail."

For Bill Surgi and the majority of those on the *Yorktown*, the day began well before dawn with the call to General Quarters. Bill had spent the night at his battle station, the airy catwalk that hung just off the starboard edge of the flight deck, aft of the No. 1 elevator. Although his mattress consisted of boxes of cables and aircraft arresting wires, it was considerably more pleasant than his hot and stuffy bunk belowdecks. As a result he didn't have far to go. "Our scout planes were about to take off. As an aviation mechanic, I had the responsibility to take care of any mechanical problems that came up. Once the planes were safely away, I went to my mess for breakfast. Then I went back to my battle station on the *Yorktown*, which was the fire station in the catwalk amidships opposite the island. There were about five of us there. Anticipating that if we got hit we would certainly have a fire, we uncoiled the fire hose—these were three inch linen hoses—so that we would be ready when the moment came."

The *Yorktown* steams into battle on the morning of June 4, 1942, with a Dauntless dive-bomber flying overhead.

Act One: The *kido butai* versus Midway

O N MIDWAY, RADIOMAN 3RD CLASS HARRY FERRIER AND SEAMAN 1ST CLASS JAY Manning had been sitting side by side inside the aft fuselage of their Avenger torpedo bomber since half an hour before dawn. Each of them wore a chambray shirt, dungaree trousers, and a life jacket, and as the sun rose the air was beginning to get stuffy in the belly of their shiny new Grumman. Besides, Ferrier and Manning were itching to get airborne. An attack on enemy ships was the biggest thing they had ever experienced.

About 0600, a Marine ran over and shouted up to the pilot, Ens. Bert Earnest: "Enemy forces at 320°, 150 miles." This was it! The Japanese fleet had been spotted. Ferrier felt the vibrations as the six Avengers' engines roared to life, the gentle jolting as their airplane taxied out onto the Eastern Island runway. His body pressed against the flight harness as the plane accelerated, and the jolts came faster. Then there was the glorious sense of release as the wheels left the ground.

All six aircraft of the Torpedo Squadron Eight detachment took off into the gentle southeasterly breeze, with Lt. Langdon Fieberling in the lead. They formed into two sections of three planes each as they made their turn to the west, climbed to cruising altitude, then adopted a course for the enemy position at a speed of 160 knots.

When their plane leveled off, Ferrier and Manning moved to their in-flight positions. Manning climbed into the turret and strapped himself into the electrically swiveling seat that faced the tail and allowed him to cover a roughly 180° arc with his single .50-caliber machine gun. From this elevated position, he could see the atoll and the other airplanes taking off from it. The radio gunner's seat was cocooned under the turret in the Grumman's belly. It faced forward and afforded only two tiny glimpses of the world outside through windows to Ferrier's right and left. Once strapped in, he made sure his radio was properly tuned to the Midway command frequency, then settled back to wait for something to happen.

The six planes were floating along above scattered clouds like Sunday fliers when an enemy aircraft swooped down on them seemingly from out of nowhere—probably a Japanese fighter, or "bandit" in military parlance. "We knew the plane was from the force on its way to Midway," Ferrier remembers. "So we knew that something was really going to happen. This was no drill." The visit was over almost as quickly as it had begun. Moments later, Manning's voice came over the intercom that connected pilot, turret gunner, and radio gunner. He reported that he could see gun flashes and puffs of smoke over the atoll.

THE 108 PLANES OF LT. JOICHI TOMONAGA'S STRIKE FORCE APPROACHED MIDWAY IN A SOLID MASS of perfect V-formations, with the fighters trailing overhead at between 11,000 and 12,000 feet. (Before the attack one Kate from *Hiryu* turned back due to engine trouble, leaving 107.) The attacking force comprised 36 Nakajima B5N2 Type 97 torpedo bombers, later codenamed Kates by the Americans; 36 Aichi D3A 1 Type 99 dive-bombers, later codenamed Vals; and 36 Mitsubishi A6M2 Type 0 fighters, later code-named Zekes, but more often referred to as Zeros. As the Japanese were beginning their final approach the American Marine fighters rose to meet them. The Midway defenders did considerable damage to the lead Japanese formations, but they were too greatly outnumbered to stave off the attack, which hit Sand and Eastern Islands with devastating force. Antiaircraft fire from ground batteries brought down more Japanese planes, but the majority managed to drop their bombs and head for home.

Filming it all from atop the powerhouse on Sand Island was John Ford, the famous movie director turned military documentary maker. During the attack he was briefly knocked unconscious by a piece of shrapnel from a bomb that exploded nearby. When he woke up, he continued filming even though one arm was full of shrapnel. As a result, we have a priceless motion picture record of the Japanese attack on Midway.

John Ford's
Battle of Midway

Celebrated Hollywood director John Ford was in the thick of it when the Japanese attacked on the morning of June 4, 1942. Ford, serving as a commander in the navy, had arrived at Midway a few days before the attack. Working as his own cameraman, he caught the Japanese attack on film, recording bomb after bomb landing around him, until one blast knocked him unconscious. His camera, still rolling, dropped from his hands. Said Ford of Midway's defenders: "I have never seen a greater exhibition of courage and coolness under fire in my life and I have seen some in my day. Those kids were really remarkable." Ford's resulting film, *Battle of Midway*, captured that spirit, as one of the very first films made on a real battlefield and with only real combatants before the lens. It won the 1942 Academy Award for best documentary.

"The enemy's attack was the simplest they could have made....They were in one group and they came straight in to the target."

—Lt. Col. Ira E. Kimes, commander of the Marine Aircraft Group on Midway, June 4, 1942

Midway's defenders were no match for the Japanese force that hit the atoll. As the painting (left) by war artist John Hamilton shows, the obsolescent Brewster Buffalo fighters manned by the Marine flyers didn't have a hope against the speedy Japanese Zeros. The Japanese left the airfield (below) intact, but successfully targeted other key installations such as the fuel tanks (above). (Top) U.S. marines raise the flag during the bombing.

"WE HAD BEEN FLYING FOR ABOUT AN HOUR," SAYS HARRY FERRIER, "so it was about seven o'clock in the morning when Bert Earnest called over the intercom: 'I can see ships ahead of us.'" He counted two aircraft carriers. Ferrier quickly crawled behind his seat and knelt at the .30-caliber tunnel gun. He could see nothing but distant water through the narrow aft-facing aperture that angled just below the airplane's tail. He had barely assumed his position when "Jay Manning called out that we were being attacked by Japanese fighters."

All six Midway-based planes of Torpedo Eight dived at full throttle in an attempt to shake off the nimble Japanese Zeros. With their own guns firing and the enemy bullets raining on their fuselages like hail hitting a tin roof, the men found the noise deafening. Wave after wave of Zeros swarmed in, and one by one, the Avengers fell. Out the tiny window to his left, Ferrier saw a burning airplane streak by, then disappear into a cloud. The noise of firing from the turret gunner stopped. He looked over his shoulder to see why. Manning was hanging limp in his harness.

"The sight of Jay's slumped and lifeless body startled me," Ferrier later wrote. "Quite suddenly, I was a scared, mature old man of 18. (In reality, Ferrier was still 17, but he stuck to his falsified age until he retired from the Navy.) I had never seen death before, and here in one awesome moment my friends and I were face to face with it. I lost all sense of time and direction but huddled by my gun, hoping for a chance to shoot back." His gun soon became useless when an enemy shell knocked out the hydraulic system for the tail wheel, which dropped and blocked his line of fire.

A few moments later, Ferrier felt a searing pain in his wrist. Then a stunning blow to his head knocked him unconscious.

"The next thing I remember was waking up with my head hanging down and blood pouring down my face. I stuck my hand up there. It almost felt like I could stick my finger into a hole. At that point I was wondering if I was going to die. I was wearing a baseball cap at the time and when I looked at it later, it had two holes: the hole where the bullet went in and the one where the bullet came out. After some moments, I decided that maybe I wasn't going to die after all."

His wrist still hurt horribly, but the wound to his head was barely noticeable.

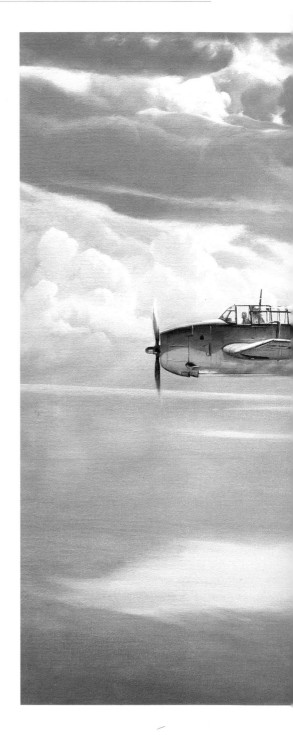

Japanese Zeros pounce on the six Midway-based Grumman Avengers of Torpedo Squadron Eight as they near the Japanese fleet. Harry Ferrier's plane is in the foreground. The rear wheel, hit by a Japanese shell, hangs down limply.

Meanwhile the man in the pilot's seat had pretty much abandoned hope of keeping his aircraft aloft. Bert Earnest's neck bled profusely from a shallow wound, and he had lost elevator control. As far as he knew, both of his crew were dead. Nonetheless, he had managed to drop his torpedo in the general direction of a destroyer or light cruiser before bracing himself for the crash. Instinctively he rolled back the elevator tab as he would in attempting to bring the nose up just before a landing. Miraculously the plane leaped upward. Then two Zeros jumped him. As more machine-gun bullets poured into the fuselage, he kept flying to the west, away from the Japanese fleet. Finally, "after what seemed like hours, but was probably less than five minutes, the Zeros left."

With his compass out of commission, Ensign Earnest would have to feel his way home. To avoid a second encounter with the Japanese, who now lay between him and Midway, he turned south. Suddenly Ferrier's voice crackled over the intercom, informing him that the turret gunner was dead but that his own wound seemed superficial. The radioman climbed forward and got into the seat behind him.

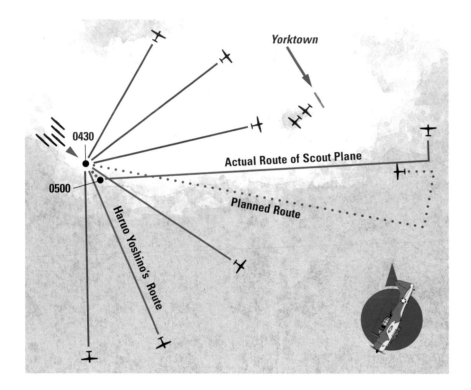

It has been called one of history's great "what-ifs." If the Japanese scout plane that spotted the American fleet had not taken off 30 minutes late from the cruiser *Tone*, Admiral Nagumo would have learned about the American carriers that much earlier, rearmed his planes faster, and perhaps carried the day for Japan. In fact *Tone*'s scout plane saw the Americans only because it had veered far off course to the north (solid line). Had *Tone*'s plane departed as scheduled and flown its proper course (the dotted line), it would have missed the enemy entirely. (One Japanese scout that morning actually managed to fly right over the American fleet and not see it.)

Judging that he was now safely south of the Japanese fleet, Earnest turned his plane east into the sun, which was now halfway up the morning sky. It filled his cockpit with light but not much warmth—all the bullet holes made for more than enough air conditioning. He didn't even need to crack the cockpit window.

ADMIRAL NAGUMO WAS NOT HAVING A GOOD MORNING, DESPITE THE APPARENT SUCCESS OF HIS Midway strike and the fact that his fleet had dodged every bomb and torpedo launched at it by successive waves of airplanes from Midway. First had come the news from his strike leader, Lt. Joichi Tomonaga: "There is need for a second attack wave." In response, the Japanese admiral ordered his remaining planes, which had been held in reserve in case an enemy fleet materialized, to switch from anti-ship torpedoes to bombs. Then one of his scout planes radioed that it had discovered "what appears to be ten enemy surface ships." At last Nagumo's question "But where is the enemy fleet?" appeared to have been answered. Exactly what sort of fleet he faced remained an open question. He could not imagine that this force included even one aircraft carrier, but just to be on the safe side, he ordered those planes that had not yet switched from torpedoes to retain them. When there was a moment between American attacks, he dispatched a message to the scout plane that had sent this infuriatingly vague report: "Ascertain ship types and maintain contact." The scout plane's first response to this directive was reassuring: "Enemy is composed of five cruisers and five destroyers."

Now, at 0820, just as the returning Midway attack force was passing over the

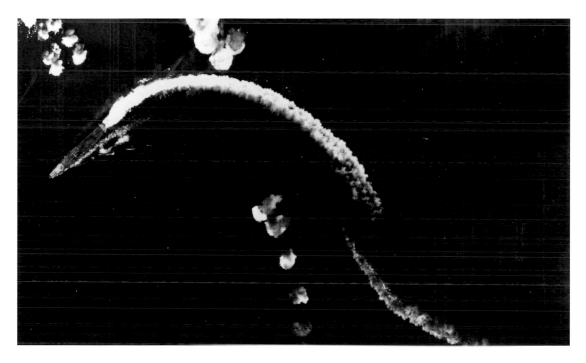

The *Hiryu* maneuvers violently during a high-level attack from Flying Fortresses.

outskirts of his fleet, which was still dodging the last of the American Midway-based attackers, the scout plane changed its tune. The enemy fleet included "what appears to be a carrier." Regardless, Nagumo's hands were tied for the moment. He could not launch a striking force until the last enemy bomber had been chased off. Nor did he wish to send out his own bombers without fighters to protect them. His first order of business was to recover the returning planes from the morning's attack on Midway before they ran out of fuel.

Accordingly, he ordered the partially armed second attack wave moved back down below to the hangar decks of his four carriers. As the crewmen hastily carried out this order, they left fuel lines and munitions littering the decks, making the ships potential powder kegs. Anxiously he paced up and down on the *Akagi*'s bridge, periodically scanning the sky for any sign of carrier-based airplanes. If only he could get his planes into the air before the Americans found him.

"WE BOTH SAW A BIG COLUMN OF BLACK SMOKE COMING UP INTO THE SKY AND REALIZED WE'D found our way home," says Harry Ferrier. "Soon we saw the atoll. There was a lot of damage, but the runways looked fine. Because the Japs had shot out our hydraulic system, Bert dropped the landing gear by the emergency system. He had no wing flaps, and he couldn't close his bomb doors. All he had was limited elevator control. But he didn't know that only one wheel had come down.

"The first time we came in, the ground crew waved us off. We came around and they waved us off again. I guess they saw we had only one wheel. The third

time Bert said, 'I'm going to land whether they like it or not.'

"He brought us in fairly smoothly, but as soon as that one wheel hit the runway and we began to lose airspeed, the wingtip dropped. It hit the runway and sent us into a spin. We came to a stop at the edge of the tarmac. I popped the canopy and crawled out of my seat. I was covered with blood. They put me into a field ambulance and carted me off to an underground field hospital. I remember the doctor telling me that my head wound was superficial. He just shaved the hair off, cleaned it, put a bandage on it and sent me on my way. I had a hell of a headache, but I was still walking around."

Earnest and Ferrier were the only members from the Midway detachment of the Torpedo Eight air crew to survive their squadron's attack on the *kido butai*.

The other 5 planes and their 16 comrades had all been lost. Their story was typical. The early morning attack from Midway had been disastrous for the Americans. Of the 51 planes sent against the Japanese carriers, only 33 returned, including all 14 of the ineffectual Boeing B17Es, or Flying Fortresses. The Japanese, on the other hand, lost only 9 planes during the bombing of Midway and left behind them considerable destruction.

The columns of black smoke that led Earnest and Ferrier home came from direct hits on three oil storage tanks on Midway's Sand Island. On Eastern Island, the power

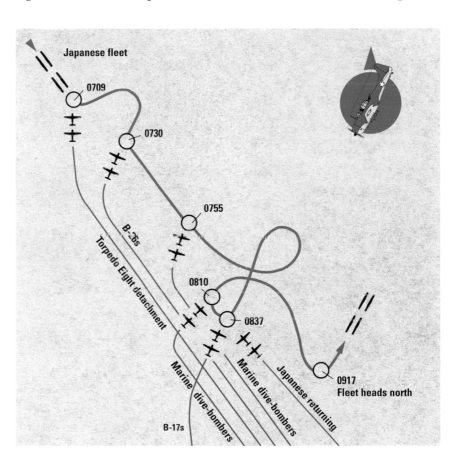

Harry Ferrier's battered Avenger (opposite) after his wing-and-a-prayer landing on Midway. The following day he collected a souvenir, the lanyard Bert Earnest had tugged to start their torpedo. (Right) Torpedo Fight was just one of the Midway-based units sent against the Japanese. As the Japanese planes flew home, Marine dive-bombers and Army B17Es and B-26s attacked their carriers—without success.

plant had been destroyed, as had gasoline lines leading from the main fuel storage. Japanese bombs had demolished a number of buildings and damaged others on both islands, but it was the damage to the fuel tanks and lines that posed the greatest potential problem. The few craters in the runways, which do not seem to have been primary Japanese targets, were easily repaired. Presumably the attackers expected them soon to be in Japanese hands and launching Japanese planes.

For their awful sacrifice, the American fliers had earned no tangible result. Although the Army pilots claimed heavy damage, not a single bomb or torpedo had hit a single Japanese ship. At the end of this first phase of the Battle of Midway, the tide ran heavily in favor of the Japanese.

The two carriers of Admiral Spruance's Task Force 16: the *Enterprise* as she looked in 1944 (above) and the *Hornet* (below). Both could carry nearly a hundred aircraft. (Opposite) Devastator torpedo bombers from the *Enterprise*'s air group parked on the aft end of the ship's flight deck.

Act Two: The Carrier Battle Begins

WHEN WORD OF THE TWO JAPANESE CARRIERS' POSITION REACHED THE AMERICAN fleet, the *Yorktown* was waiting to recover the scout planes it had launched at dawn. Determined to engage the enemy at the earliest opportunity, Admiral Fletcher ordered his second in command to "proceed southwesterly and attack enemy carriers as soon as definitely located. I will follow as soon as planes recovered." Until the situation clarified, Fletcher would keep his options open by holding his own airplanes in reserve. At Coral Sea, he had sent his entire force after a target identified as two aircraft carriers, only to discover the ships were cruisers. He couldn't afford to make such a mistake again. Adm. Raymond Spruance and his two carriers, the *Enterprise* and the *Hornet*, would have the honor of sending off the first carrier planes against the Japanese fleet.

As Spruance's two carriers charged southwestward at high speed, the admiral and his staff debated when they would be close enough to the calculated enemy position to begin launching. Spruance hoped to surprise the enemy with its planes down—its Midway attack force on deck and in the midst of refueling. But if he sent his attack

off too soon, he risked losing many of his fliers on the return flight. The shorter range of his fighters and torpedo bombers was the limiting factor. Complicating matters, the wind was blowing gently from the southeast. When it came time to launch, a process that would take at least half an hour, he would have to steam in the opposite direction from the enemy.

By 0700, just as Harry Ferrier and the rest of his group had approached the expected vicinity of the Japanese fleet, the *Enterprise* and the *Hornet* had begun launching. The *Hornet*'s squadrons took off without a hitch, but on the *Enterprise*, the process was agonizingly slow. According to Lt. Comdr. Wade McClusky, who watched the final planes being spotted (positioned for takeoff) on the *Enterprise*'s flight deck as he circled above, "Action seemed to come to a standstill." Finally, at 0745, Admiral Spruance felt he could wait no longer. The first airplanes launched had been airborne for more than half an hour, all the time wasting precious fuel. He ordered those planes already aloft to make for the Japanese, which meant that they left without the fighter escort still sitting on the *Enterprise*'s deck. The *Hornet*'s air group, meanwhile, had flown off on its chosen heading. (Each carrier group drew its own conclusion, based on its own calculation of where the enemy was.) By the time *(continued on page 76)*

Nose to Nose

At the Battle of Midway, three types of carrier-launched airplane were used by each side: single-seat fighters, and dive-bombers and torpedo bombers carrying two or three crew members.

Japan's greatest apparent advantage lay in its fighters: the Zero outclassed the Wildcat in speed and maneuverability, making it virtually unbeatable in a one-on-one dogfight, but its lack of protective armor made it vulnerable. At Midway, Wildcats shot down Zeros at a rate of two to one.

The torpedo bombers on both sides fared poorly during the battle due to the slow, shallow approach they needed to make a successful torpedo launch. But at least the Japanese could count on effective torpedoes. If any American torpedoes found their targets, none exploded.

The Americans owed their offensive success at Midway almost entirely to their dive-bombers. The U.S. Navy's sturdy Dauntlesses could roar down on a target at an angle so steep that they were almost impossible to shoot down, then buzz away before anyone could retaliate.

MITSUBISHI A6M "ZEKE" OR "ZERO"

Type: single-seat fighter
Armament: two 7.7 mm machine guns, two 20 mm cannon; sometimes two 130 lb bombs

Range: 1,160 miles; maximum: 1,930 miles
Speed: cruising: 207 mph; maximum: 330 mph

GRUMMAN F4F-4 "WILDCAT"

Type: single-seat carrier fighter
Armament: six .50 cal machine guns

Range: 910 miles
Speed: cruising: 148 mph; maximum: 312 mph

NAKAJIMA B5N2 TYPE 97 CARRIER BOMBER "KATE"

Type: three-seat attack bomber
Armament: one pivotable stern-mounted 7.7 mm machine gun; one 1,760 lb

torpedo or bombs of same weight
Range: 608 miles
Speed: cruising: 161 mph; maximum: 235 mph

DOUGLAS TBD-1 "DEVASTATOR"

Type: three- (later two-) seat torpedo bomber
Armament: one forward-firing .30 cal machine gun, one or two pivotable stern-

mounted .30 cal machine gun; one 2,000 lb torpedo
Range: 716 miles
Speed: cruising: 128 mph; maximum: 206 mph

AICHI D3A1/2 TYPE 99 CARRIER BOMBER "VAL"

Type: two-seat carrier dive-bomber
Armament: two forward-firing 7.7 mm machine guns, one pivotable stern-mounted 7.7 mm machine

gun; one 550 lb bomb under fuselage, or two 130 lb bombs under each wing
Range: 915 miles
Speed: cruising: 184 mph; maximum: 240 mph

DOUGLAS SBD-2/-3 "DAUNTLESS"

Type: two-seat scout/dive-bomber
Armament: two forward-firing .50 cal machine guns, two pivotable stern-mounted .30 cal machine guns; up to 1,000 lb in

bombs, or, typically, one 500 lb bomb plus two 150 lb bombs under each wing
Range: 1,205 miles
Speed: cruising: 144 mph; maximum: 245 mph

(continued from page 73) the last planes had left the *Enterprise*, formed up, and flown off to the southwest, Admiral Spruance's vision of a coordinated attack had disintegrated into three separate groups, only one of which included its intended fighter escort of Grumman F4F-4 Wildcats.

However disorganized the force might be that the carriers had launched, in all, 116 American bombers, torpedo planes, and fighters were heading toward the estimated Japanese position, marginally more than the number Admiral Nagumo had earlier launched against Midway.

(Top) This photograph of the *Kaga* from the early 1930s clearly reveals her origin as a battleship refitted to carry a flight deck. In 1935, the flight deck was extended forward and an island superstructure added. At Midway she more closely resembled the *Akagi* (above), which had originally been laid down as a battle cruiser. Capable of speeds of up to 30 knots, both ships escaped any damage from American torpedo bombers.

PETTY OFFICER 3RD CLASS YUJI AKAMATSU HAD SPENT THE HOURS SINCE DAWN IN THE observer/navigator's seat of a Kate on antisubmarine patrol ahead of the fleet. As his plane returned to the *Kaga* to refuel, he found the Japanese carriers in the midst of an American assault. "As we approached, six departing American planes attacked us," he recalls, "but they didn't stay for long. We had to circle the fleet for quite a while before it was possible to land. Our carriers were turning left and right to avoid the enemy bombs. We could not land until the *Kaga* headed into the wind. Finally, our fighters drove off the last American planes and we were able to land."

Akamatsu's return to the flight deck of the *Kaga* seems to have roughly coincided with the return of the airplanes from Lieutenant Tomonaga's Midway attack force. As soon as these planes were recovered, they were hastily moved below to the hangar deck while the fueled and armed second attack wave was brought up. Meanwhile

Akamatsu headed for his ready room and a late breakfast of rice, soy bean soup, raw eggs, pickles, and tea. When he and his comrades heard the first reports of the raid on Midway, they had reason to eat with satisfaction. Total Japanese losses amounted to only 9 of the 107 planes that had made it all the way to the atoll, and the damage seemed to have been heavy. By any standard the attack had been a great success.

On the bridge of the *Akagi*, Admiral Nagumo watched impatiently as his four carriers plowed north–northeast at 30 knots. In a matter of minutes, he would be ready to launch an all-out attack on the lone American aircraft carrier his scout plane had spotted. Once it was out of action, he would finish off the stubborn but by now badly hammered American defenders on Midway.

At 0920, with the last of the Midway attack force recovered, the *Akagi*'s bridge received reports of approaching enemy planes. As the reports multiplied, Nagumo began to suspect that this force comprised more planes than could have come from a single enemy carrier. Suddenly, all the admiral's assumptions, all his careful command decisions, were thrown into doubt. If the enemy fleet consisted of two or more carriers, he was in for a very different sort of battle than he had anticipated. Understanding that he must counterattack as quickly as possible, he issued the order, "Speed preparations for immediate takeoff," but it was a command impossible to execute. All four of his carriers had their hands full dodging the seemingly endless waves of enemy attacks. And as soon as there was a break in the action, his first order of business would be to recover the fighters flying combat air patrol. They were running low on fuel and ammunition and would need to be relieved before any striking force could sanely be launched. Nagumo was in a box, and one that was partly of his own making.

FIRST ON THE SCENE WAS THE *HORNET*'S TORPEDO SQUADRON, THE CARRIER-BASED COMPONENT of Harry Ferrier's Torpedo Squadron Eight. Thus, by strange coincidence, the first carrier-based planes to attack the Japanese fleet came from the same squadron as the first Midway-based attackers. Ens. George Gay acted as Torpedo Eight's navigator, which meant he flew last and on the outside wing so as to concentrate on his job and not worry about flying close formation. From this position, he had all too clear a view of the fate of his comrades.

"Zeros were coming in from all angles and from both sides at once. They would come in from abeam, pass each other just over our heads, and turn around to make another attack. It was evident that they were trying to get our lead planes first. The planes of Torpedo Eight were falling at irregular intervals. Some were on fire, and some did a half roll and crashed on their backs, completely out of control. Machine-gun bullets ripped my armor plate a number of times. As they rose above it, the bullets would go over my shoulder into the instrument panel, and through the windshield."

The squadron commander, Lt. Comdr. John C. Waldron, was one of the Zeros' first victims. With his plane on fire, he struggled to climb out of his cockpit but had only his right leg free before he crashed into the water and disappeared.

Gay's radio gunner's voice came over the intercom. "They got me."

Gay looked aft to see his one crewman slumped over, obviously hurt badly.

"Can you move?" Gay demanded.

There was no answer.

During this brief interlude, another plane had been shot down. Gay, who that day had taken off from a carrier deck with a torpedo for the very first time, began to dodge and weave, trying anything to elude the attackers. More of his squadron fell. A bullet hit him softly in the arm. He squeezed it out like popping a pimple and stuck it in his mouth. Well, what do you know, he thought, a souvenir.

Including his plane, only three of the squadron were still flying as they turned toward the carrier chosen as their target. Gay maneuvered sharply to avoid another Zero. When he turned back, one of the other two planes was gone; the second had been hit and was diving out of control. Torpedo Squadron Eight now consisted of Ensign Gay's plane alone.

He was preparing to drop his torpedo when something slammed into the back of his left hand. "It hurt like hell." Somehow he managed to pull back on the throttle with his left thumb to level the plane for a torpedo drop. One thousand yards range, 80 knots of speed, about 80 feet of altitude. Perfect. He punched the release button. Nothing happened.

"I almost lost control of the plane trying to pull out that cable by the roots," Gay later recalled of his attempt to drop the torpedo manually. "I can't honestly say if I got rid of that torpedo. It felt like it. I had never done it before, so I couldn't be sure, and with the plane pitching like a bronco I had to be content with trying my best."

With or without his torpedo he was now screaming toward the eye of the Japanese hurricane through a storm of flak and fighter fire with no real option but to fly right over the enemy carrier. At least the Zeros wouldn't follow him there. He flew along

A Douglas Devastator under fire after launching its torpedo. Whether because of stiff Japanese resistance or defective torpedoes, no American torpedo bombers inflicted any damage during the battle.

a flight deck crowded with planes and men, turned left at the stern, and headed between two cruisers, flying as low as possible. By the time he reached the outer ring of destroyers, more Zeros awaited him.

One slug shot out his rudder pedal, passing within a fraction of an inch of his little toe, tearing through the fire wall and setting the engine ablaze. He still had sufficient elevator control to level the plane for a liquid landing. He almost managed it, too, until a crosswind dipped his right wing. The plane did a cartwheel, twisting its frame as it slammed against the water and wedging the cockpit hood shut.

By the time George Gay had unbuckled his flight harness, the water was up to his waist. He climbed up onto the instrument panel and tried to open the hood. "When the water got up to my armpits and started lapping at my chin, I got scared—and I mean really scared. I knew the plane would dive as soon as it lost buoyancy, and I didn't want to drown in there. I panicked, stood up, and busted my way out."

IN THE PILOTS' READY ROOM ABOARD THE *KAGA*, YUJI AKAMATSU WAS just tucking into breakfast when Torpedo Eight was sighted. "An alarm sounded signaling an air raid, so I stopped eating and went up on deck. The first wave of planes had come in to attack, but we had expected this and sent out the fighter planes. Because we were attack specialists, we were interested in what kind of attack the Americans would use. They appeared at least 4,000 or 5,000 meters off, and approached at a low altitude of 100 to 150 meters. They dropped their torpedoes from quite a distance, so the bridge had lots of time to take evasive maneuvers.

(Above) Ens. George Gay. (Below) A Devastator torpedo bomber ditches near the American destroyer *Monaghan*. Of the three torpedo bomber squadrons present at Midway, almost all of the slow-moving Devastators were lost.

"Their method was quite different from the training we had received. We would come in very close. At 1,000 meters, I would give the signal to drop. When we released our torpedoes, we were just 800 meters away. That's why we hit our targets almost 100 percent of the time. However, it is also why we were shot down almost 100 percent of the time."

Aboard the *Akagi*, Comdr. Mitsuo Fuchida watched the fiery fate of Torpedo Eight while lying flat on the flight deck. The next raid was not long in coming, this time far more serious in nature.

"Enemy torpedo bombers, 30° to starboard, coming in low!" shouted the lookout atop the bridge.

"Enemy torpedo planes approaching 40° to port!"

Fuchida watched in a state of high suspense as the dangerous two-pronged attack unfolded. Finally the Americans were getting smart. It seemed unthinkable that the

Torpedo Squadron Eight

Following the battle of Midway, John Ford met with Capt. Marc Mitscher, then commander of the carrier *Hornet*. A forward-thinking officer, Mitscher routinely had many of the *Hornet*'s operations filmed, and Ford wanted footage for his Midway movie. Mitscher agreed—with one condition: that the director also create a film commemorating the *Hornet*-based members of Torpedo Squadron Eight, whose annihilation at Midway—only George Gay survived—weighed on Mitscher.

The resulting seven-and-a-half-minute film, accompanied only by a musical score, features captions introducing Torpedo Eight's fliers, who are shown posed poignantly in group shots or smiling self-consciously in front of their obsolescent Devastators. The film also shows footage of the squadron's planes aboard the *Hornet* at the Coral Sea—and taking off for the last time on the morning of Midway. Thirty copies of the 35 mm film were made, for the families of those who died June 4th and for the lone survivor, Gay. The film was never shown commercially, and many accounts of Ford's career fail to mention it. The pictures here, published for the first time, were made from frames cut from one print of the film.

(Below left) Crewmen push a Devastator, its wings still folded for storage but armed with a torpedo, along the deck of the *Hornet*. (Below right) A Devastator readies for takeoff. (Above) All the pilots of the *Hornet*'s Torpedo Squadron Eight pose on the flight deck at the time of the Battle of the Coral Sea. George Gay is the fourth man from the left in the first row.

Akagi could dodge so many torpedoes. But once again the attackers had arrived without fighter escort. Once again the Zeros engaged the enemy and once again the torpedo planes began to fall.

"On the *Akagi*'s flight deck, all attention was fixed on the dramatic scene unfolding before us, and there was wild cheering and whistling as the raiders went down one after another."

In the end only five or six American planes survived to launch their torpedoes, but the angles were so poor and the Japanese carriers handled so deftly that all the torpedoes sailed harmlessly by.

Although this second attack appeared to Fuchida to consist of 40 enemy planes, it comprised only the 14 Douglas TBD-1 torpedo bombers, or Devastators, of the *Enterprise*'s Torpedo Squadron Six under the leadership of Lt. Comdr. Eugene E. Lindsey. Four of Lindsey's planes returned to their carrier, but his was not among them. One wonders how much better they would have fared had he made contact with the *Enterprise*'s ten Wildcat fighters under Lt. James Gray that had arrived first over the *kido butai*. Gray was holding position just ahead of the fleet's course while attempting to contact Lindsey by radio. The two torpedo attacks unfolded without his knowledge, since he failed to pick up Lindsey's radio requests for fighter support. Just after 1000, with its fuel running low, Gray's flight turned for home.

Paradoxically the defeat of the carrier-launched torpedo bombers left Admiral Nagumo in a precarious position. His decks remained crowded with the planes meant for an attack on the U.S. fleet, making them highly explosive targets for enemy bombers. Many of his combat air patrol of fighters had run low on ammunition and had to be landed before he could launch. Chasing off the torpedo attack had left those fighters remaining in the air at low altitudes.

On the American side of the ledger, there was little to bolster confidence. The launch of Rear Admiral Spruance's attacking force had been inefficient and confused. Many of his planes had failed to find the Japanese at all. None of those that actually arrived did so with their assigned fighter escort. Of the 29 torpedo bombers sent against the enemy, only four returned. Not a single hit was scored. When they returned, finding their ship posed a whole new challenge. Spruance's staff had neglected to properly calculate Point Option—the estimated course and speed of the carrier while its launched aircraft were away—information that allowed returning planes to speedily locate their home carrier. Spruance looked in serious danger of becoming the whipping boy of Midway.

As the second act of the Battle of Midway came to a close, the balance was still weighted heavily in Nagumo's favor. Not one of his ships had been touched, the majority of his planes were still operational, and the cost to the Americans in terms of both aircraft and men had been heavy. But the commanding Japanese admiral now knew that he faced at least one, and probably more than one, American flattop, which meant that his troubles were just beginning.

Act Three: Six Fatal Minutes

S O FAR, THE MORNING HAD BEEN UNEVENTFUL FOR PETTY OFFICER 1ST CLASS HARUO Yoshino, commander of the lone scout plane launched from the *Kaga* that day. Yoshino occupied the middle, or observer's, seat. Unlike the American practice, the pilot was often not the aircraft commander. As he approached the position where he expected to find the Japanese fleet, he still knew nothing of the recent attacks by American torpedo bombers on the *kido butai*.

"As I passed over Kure Island [60 miles northwest of Midway] and flew westward, I spotted four planes that looked like American planes. Usually when four planes fly together they are in standard formation, but these four were flying separately and almost at sea level, heading east. I immediately realized that our fleet had been under attack."

As he approached the carriers, he saw to his relief that the *Kaga* and the other three seemed unharmed, although their tight formation had been broken by all the high-speed maneuvering during the morning battles, with the *Hiryu* now steaming well to the north of the other three. By pure coincidence, Yoshino seems to have arrived home in a brief lull between torpedo plane attacks.

"I didn't have to wait long before the flight crew on board the *Kaga* raised the flag indicating that it was safe to land. As soon as I brought my plane safely down, I reported to the captain, but he wasn't interested in hearing my report. He told me that another enemy force was approaching, so I went down into my ready room."

(Top) Aboard the *Yorktown,* a line of Dauntlesses prepares for takeoff. (Above) Lt. Comdr. Jimmy Thach sits in the cockpit of his Wildcat fighter. The small Japanese flags on the plane's side represent enemy aircraft shot down.

ADMIRAL FLETCHER ON BOARD THE *YORKTOWN* HAD WAITED AS LONG AS HE could before finally launching against the enemy just after 0830. As soon as his search planes were recovered, he had raced southwest toward the Japanese fleet, but he did not want to commit even part of his force until all the Japanese carriers had been found. Ever conscious of the larger picture, and of the lessons of Coral Sea, he chose to launch a limited strike, holding in reserve one dive-bombing squadron. Neither he nor Admiral Spruance yet knew just how many Japanese carriers they faced, or whether the enemy comprised a single carrier force or several. (Thanks to the breaking of the Japanese naval code, Fletcher did have an intelligence report that predicted four or five aircraft carriers in the attacking Japanese force.) He wanted to be ready to take on any new target if and when it became available.

Nonetheless, he sent off a formidable attack fleet: 12 Devastator torpedo bombers, 17 Douglas SBD, or Dauntless, dive-bombers, and 6 escorting Wildcats. Leading the fighter contingent was Lt. Comdr. Jimmy Thach, formerly of the *Saratoga*

and the *Lexington*, one of the most experienced and innovative fighter commanders in the U.S. Navy. Thach had drilled some of his young pilots in a new tactic: the "beam defense," a technique in which two airplanes wove simultaneously back and forth so as to prevent a pursuing Zero from ever fixing one as a target. After the Battle of Midway, it would be known as the Thach Weave.

Bill Surgi watched *Yorktown*'s launch from his battle station. When he stood in the catwalk, his shoulders were just about level with the flight deck, so he had an amazing wheel-level view of the planes racing by, only about 30 feet away. It was exhilarating to see his personal Airedales, the pilots of Fighter Squadron Three, take to the air as the torpedo squadron's escort.

While the *Yorktown*'s first strike winged its way toward the scene of battle, the

Dauntless dive-bombers silhouetted against a rising sun. The plane was designed with an enclosed cockpit, but on active operations crews typically flew with the plane "opened up" to the elements. The radio man/gunner was equipped with a machine gun (later two), to ward off marauding enemy fighters.

dive-bombers from the *Enterprise* and the *Hornet* were still searching for the Japanese fleet—which wasn't where they expected it to be.

The day was going especially poorly for the *Hornet*'s bomber group. First, their fighter escort was forced to turn back when their fuel levels became critically low. About 0920, when the dive-bombers reached the predicted intercept point, they found themselves flying above scattered clouds over a stretch of empty ocean. Having no clear plan where to look for the Japanese, they simply continued westward, while their radio receivers crackled with the sounds of the torpedo bombers at battle. Now it was the bombers' fuel that was dropping dangerously low. The group began to break apart, as first one squadron, then another, turned for home. Some chose to land on Midway. Most made it back to their ships.

Likewise, the *Enterprise*'s force of 33 dive-bombers, under the command of Lt. Comdr. Wade McClusky, arrived at an empty point of intercept. But unlike his *Hornet* confrères, McClusky had a plan for finding the Japanese. First he scouted west, then turned northwest on a reciprocal bearing to the last known course of the Japanese fleet. He assumed, correctly, that Nagumo had turned around after recovering his Midway attack force. Instead of reversing his course, however, Nagumo had headed northeast to keep within easy striking distance of Midway.

A few minutes before 1000, as McClusky was about to turn east for the last leg of his search, he spotted the wake of a ship high-tailing it to the northeast. This was the Japanese destroyer *Arashi*, which had stayed behind the fleet to give chase to the *Nautilus*, the only American submarine to have challenged the Japanese so far. The *Arashi* pointed McClusky's bombers straight to their target.

FOR A SECOND TIME, YUJI AKAMATSU INTERRUPTED HIS BREAKFAST TO witness a torpedo attack. He was appalled at the poor quality of antiaircraft fire, so he personally took charge of one of the guns. "They didn't know to fire in front of the airplanes. That was why all their shots were missing," he says.

Akamatsu now witnessed the sacrifice of the final squadron of carrier-launched torpedo planes sent against the Japanese, the *Yorktown*'s Torpedo Squadron Three. (The *Yorktown* pilots, who had left their ship more than an hour after their counterparts left the *Enterprise* and the *Hornet*, had correctly second-guessed Japanese ship movements and found the fleet in short order.)

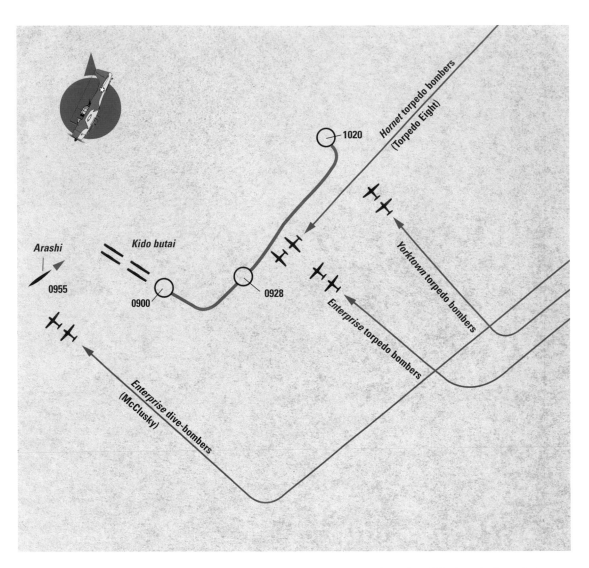

1020

Hornet torpedo bombers
(Torpedo Eight)

Arashi

Kido butai

0955

0900

0928

Yorktown torpedo bombers

Enterprise torpedo bombers

Enterprise dive-bombers
(McClusky)

Three waves of torpedo planes from the American carriers attacked the *kido butai*—but their attacks were uncoordinated, no targets were hit, and losses were heavy. Then at 0955, while searching for the enemy, *Enterprise*'s dive-bombers spotted the destroyer *Arashi* heading north.

Unlike the previous torpedo attacks, this one actually had a fighter escort. But Jimmy Thach's six Wildcats were able to distract the Zeros only temporarily. Ten of the *Yorktown*'s 12 torpedo planes went down in flames before they could hit any of the carriers. (The other two ditched near their own carriers.)

Akamatsu joined in the cheering as the American enemy planes fell like flies. Once this third wave had been repulsed, he again turned for the ready room and what was by now a very cold repast.

"As I was going down, I heard the scream of a quick-falling bomb. Oh, no, I thought. And when I looked up, I saw bombs falling in clusters. I knew this was trouble. I rushed to my ready room, expecting to be ordered to take off immediately."

As he got there, the *Kaga* was rocked by a terrible explosion.

GEORGE GAY HAD GRABBED HIS SEAT CUSHION AS HIS PLANE SANK. THE CUSHION GAVE HIM something to cling to and a place to hide from the strafing Zeros, which finally departed. As he floated in the lukewarm water, he had the only close-up view by an American combatant of the remarkable six minutes that changed the course of the Battle of Midway and of the whole Pacific War. As Gay watched from the water, he saw what looked like the entire Japanese fleet turn and steam toward him.

Wrote Gay many years later: "Then I saw why the Zeros had left me. Our dive-bombers were coming down. There is no way I can describe what a beautiful sight that was! I could see that the Zeros that had come down after us were not up there bothering them, and I knew that some of those fellows were not only pushing over in their first dive but it was also the first time they had ever flown that type of plane. They were magnificent!..."

Arriving on the heels of the *Yorktown*'s Torpedo Three came its squadron of dive-bombers under Lt. Comdr. Maxwell Leslie. By an almost miraculous coincidence, two dive-bomber groups totaling 47 planes, which had taken off from the *Enterprise* and the *Yorktown* almost two hours apart, had arrived over the Japanese fleet at the same moment and were poised to attack just when all the enemy fighters were flying low and all the enemy carriers were in a state of maximum vulnerability.

Almost simultaneously, the *Kaga*, the *Soryu*, and the *Akagi* came under dive-bomber attack. Only the *Hiryu*, now well to the north, escaped their attention. It appears the first bomb hit the *Kaga*, striking the aft end of her crowded flight deck. (The pilot, Lt. W. Earl Gallaher, couldn't resist looking back and was rewarded with the sight of flames blossoming from the enemy deck. Back on December 7, 1941, Gallaher had flown over Pearl following the Japanese attack and had seen the battleship he had served on right after graduating from Annapolis sinking and in flames. Reflexively he now said to himself, "*Arizona*, I remember you.") The second bomb hit a fuel cart on the *Kaga* just forward of the island, engulfing the bridge in a firestorm of flaming gasoline that killed the captain and everyone else there. A third bomb landed amidships, by which time the carrier was doomed.

The *Soryu* seems to have been the next victim, taking at least three hits in quick succession from the *Yorktown*'s squadron and soon becoming a mass of flames. The *Akagi*, Admiral Nagumo's proud flagship, now fell prey to the *Enterprise* attack. The first bomb went down the midships elevator and exploded on the hangar deck, where unstowed bombs and torpedoes stoked a huge inferno. One of the secondary explosions jammed the rudder.

The first bomb hit the *Kaga* at 1022; the last bomb to find the *Soryu* struck no later than 1028. Within this roughly six-minute span, all three of the Japanese carriers under attack were mortally damaged. As the dive-bombers withdrew, hotly pursued by Japanese Zeros, they could see three enemy carriers on fire. One of the retreating pilots compared the carrier he'd hit to "a haystack in flames." George Gay described the ship closest to him: "This one was burning and roaring like a giant two-headed blowtorch. Flames were sweeping through her, fore and aft, and most of her hull was red hot. It was a real inferno, and I was uneasy because I was so close."

"I HAD BARELY REACHED THE READY ROOM WHEN THE BOMBS BEGAN TO hit," remembers Yuji Akamatsu. "There were what seemed like six or seven direct hits and they came one after another. *Boom! Crash!* I was tossed in the air—I still have the scars—and I lost consciousness."

Haruo Yoshino was also in his ready room on the *Kaga* when the dive-bomber attack hit home: "I was taking off my flight suit when the first bomb went off. The whole ship shook and the noise was terrible. I rushed up to the flight deck in time to see the end of the attack. When a bomb hit near where I was standing, I threw myself on the deck. I watched the last American planes make their dives.

"The result was terrible to witness. Each bomb that hit set off more explosions. The flight deck and hangar deck were crowded with airplanes full of fuel. There were bombs and torpedoes lying everywhere. Within minutes, the ship became a sea of fire."

On the *Akagi*, Mitsuo Fuchida struggled up to the bridge as secondary explosions rocked the flagship, "shaking the bridge and filling the air with deadly splinters." In the distance, he could see that both the *Soryu* and the *Kaga* had also been hit "and were giving off heavy columns of black smoke." The *Akagi*'s "entire hangar area was a blazing inferno, and the flames moved swiftly toward the bridge."

Arriving on the bridge, he found Rear Adm. Ryunosuke Kusaka, chief of Nagumo's staff, begging the fleet commander to leave the *Akagi* and transfer his flag to the light cruiser *Nagara*. The admiral seemed dazed and disoriented. Capt. Taijiro Aoki added his voice to Kusaka's entreaties. By the time Nagumo reluctantly agreed to leave his beloved flagship, the only means of escape was via a rope ladder hanging from the forward window of the bridge. Thus did Nagumo and his staff, the emperor's portrait in tow, ignominiously abandon the aircraft carrier that had led the glorious attack against Pearl Harbor.

An attacking Dauntless dive-bomber scores the first direct hit on the *Soryu*.

"Looking about, I was horrified at the destruction that had been wrought in a matter of seconds."

—Mitsuo Fuchida,
on board the *Akagi*, June 4, 1942

Dive Bombing

The dive-bomber, or hell-diver, was the only American aircraft that the Japanese feared—and with good reason. Carrier-launched Dauntlesses sank all four Japanese flattops at Midway. But pulling off the trick of plummeting toward the sea at a dive angle of 70° or more before dropping a bomb on a small target was gut- and mind-wrenching. Harold Buell, one of the *Yorktown*'s young dive-bomber pilots, says he learned to think of the airplane as "a large rifle or cannon, with my sight the same as one on a regular gun. At the instant of release, I visualized my bomb as a bullet leaving the muzzle, moving at the velocity of my dive, and speeding to the target exactly as a bullet does when fired."

(Above and right) The steep angle of attack of a diving Dauntless. (Below) The *Kaga* on fire, in an artist's representation of the view from the *Nautilus*, the first American submarine that contacted the Japanese fleet.

NEWS OF THE STUNNING TURN IN THEIR FORTUNES REACHED THE COMMANDING AMERICAN admirals haphazardly and incompletely. While their pilots had clearly done damage to the Japanese fleet, claiming hits on three aircraft carriers, neither Fletcher nor Spruance could be certain that the three enemy ships had been permanently disabled. Reports were conflicting, but the strong possibility remained that one undamaged carrier still roamed within range of the American fleet. Fletcher and Spruance knew their force had been spotted that morning by Japanese scouts. If any Japanese carriers remained operational, an attack could be expected at any moment.

(Pages 90–91) Fires rage uncontrollably aboard the _Kaga_ as the powerless ship drifts to a complete halt, her escorts helpless to aid her.

(Right) At 1016, the _Yorktown_ and _Enterprise_'s dive-bombers met over the Japanese fleet. They attacked at 1022; by 1028, the _Kaga_, _Akagi_, and _Soryu_ were burning wrecks.

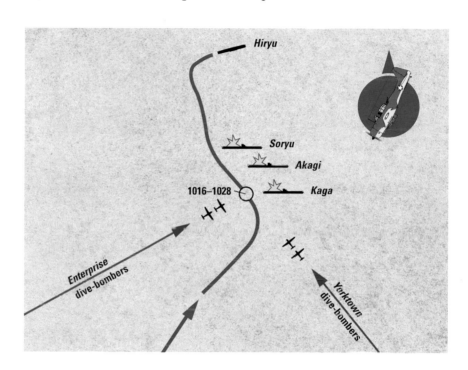

At 1130, just before the first elements of the _Yorktown_'s strike force returned from battle, Admiral Fletcher made another smart decision: He sent out a scouting mission to search for more Japanese carriers. Shortly after these planes took off, Commander Thach brought four of his five surviving Wildcats on board. (The fifth landed on the _Hornet_.) His report that "three Japanese carriers were completely out of action and that it looked like the battle was going our way," fully vindicated the "old man's" decision.

ON BOARD THE _HIRYU_, THE LONE UNSCATHED JAPANESE FLATTOP, REAR ADM. TAMON YAMAGUCHI wasted no time in launching his counterattack, even though only his bombers could get away immediately. (The torpedo planes would follow as soon as they were ready.) This talented officer, touted by some as Admiral Yamamoto's heir apparent, had long chafed under Vice Admiral Nagumo's cautious leadership. Now the field of battle was his for the taking.

Even as Nagumo was clambering down the rope ladder from the _Akagi_'s bridge, the *Hiryu* was launching its strike force against the American carrier or carriers—the commanding Japanese admiral still didn't know how many. (Reports of the number of enemy flattops varied throughout the day, adding confusion to Japanese disarray.) By 1100, barely half an hour after the devastating American dive-bomber attack, the *Hiryu*'s counterstrike was winging on its way. With it flew Japan's last hopes of salvaging some good fortune on what was already a disastrous fourth of June.

Act Four: The Japanese Counterattack

SINCE THE TAKEOFF OF THE *YORKTOWN*'S ATTACK FORCE AROUND 0830, things had been quiet, but rumors flew. As the hours passed, tension mounted. Word began to filter through the ranks that their airplanes had found the Japanese carriers and given a good account of themselves. Yet the blue Pacific sky contained nothing beyond a few high-flying clouds. Just before noon, the ship's loudspeakers began to crackle with reports relayed from the radar room of bandits approaching on bearing 255°, distance 32 miles. For only the second time in its career, and the first since the Battle of the Coral Sea a month earlier, the *Yorktown* faced an enemy air attack.

To Bill Surgi, the approaching Val dive-bombers made quite a picture against the midday sky. "Boy, they looked pretty up there," he recalled, "a good, clean-looking airplane. That would make a nice model to build, I thought to myself. And then the first one nosed over and it looked even cleaner, really sleek. He kept diving and I figured, Well, that one is going to crash into the ship. Then he released his bomb—I could see the bomb falling toward the flight deck—and he took off." The bomb crashed harmlessly into the sea, but more dive-bombers followed.

(Above) The burning *Yorktown* seen from the heavy cruiser *Pensacola*. (Opposite) Firefighters and rescue crews crowd around a 1.1-inch gun mount knocked-out during the first attack.

The first bomb to hit the *Yorktown* struck the flight deck and burst just aft of the island, near mounts Number Three and Four for the 1.1-inch anti-aircraft guns, killing 17 men, wounding 18, and sending splinter fragments down to the hangar deck where they set three planes on fire. The second bomb penetrated down to just below the second deck before exploding in fire-room uptakes and intakes. The blast completely wrecked the uptakes, disabling two boilers and blowing out the fires in another three. The third bomb sliced down the Number One elevator, exploding on the third deck, where it started a fire in a rag locker next to the storage areas for both ammunition and gasoline.

Electrician's Mate 3rd Class Gordon Skinner was lying only about 20 feet from where the first bomb hit. Even amid the ear-splitting din of antiaircraft fire, the noise struck with almost physical force, followed by a hurricane blast of air. Skinner, whose father was a fireman, had handled a fire hose before, and he was on his feet almost instantly, dragging the nozzle toward the shattered gun mount. Anticipating the broncolike buck of a hose suddenly under high pressure, Skinner dived to the deck a few feet away from the gun mount and wrapped both legs around the hose in perfect fireman fashion. An anemic stream puddled on the deck in front of him. "Put your thumb over it!" shouted a passing petty officer, busy marshaling damage-control crews. Skinner jumped up, ran forward, and did as instructed, producing a spray more suitable to a garden hose.

Each of the guns in the quadruple mount had twin seats—one for the trainer who aimed the gun and one for the pointer who fired it. One of these positions presented a grisly sight. The trainer's seat was empty, but the man in the pointer's seat was gone only from the waist up. Several men were on fire; Skinner sent his slender stream toward the one who seemed to be worst wounded—the man was trying to hold in his guts with the help of another sailor. In a few minutes, the pharmacist's mates were on hand to tend to the wounded. Skinner noticed that the vibration of the *Yorktown*'s engines had stopped; she was gliding to a halt.

In the radar room, which abutted the stack near the top of the ship's superstructure, the first blast was barely heard in the cacophony of battle. The explosion in the uptakes, however, sent shock waves upward that split the radar room's bulkhead at its

"The shock of the explosion moved the ship downward, probably three or four feet.... I would have hit the deck if I hadn't had one hand clasped against the radar transmitter."

—Radio Electrician
Vane Bennett

As black smoke pours from the *Yorktown*'s island after a bomb exploded in the fire-room uptakes, damage-control crews and medical corpsmen swarm over the deck.

seams. Soon black smoke began pouring in through the cracks. But when Radio Electrician Vane Bennett tried to open the door, he found the blast had wedged it shut. Choking from the thickening smoke, he tried desperately to break the door down. As the ship began to slow, Bennett felt certain the radar room was about to become his coffin.

ON THE *HIRYU*'S BRIDGE, ADMIRAL YAMAGUCHI GAVE FINAL INSTRUCTIONS TO THE TWO torpedo officers about to lead the second attack against the Americans. The handful of bombers that had returned from the first attack had brought with them confusing reports of the damage inflicted on one enemy carrier, but all agreed they had left the ship dead in the water. But how many other flattops did the enemy possess? One of the *Soryu*'s scout planes, whose radio had malfunctioned during its flight, provided an answer when it landed on the *Hiryu*'s deck: The enemy had "three carriers: the *Enterprise*, the *Hornet*, and the *Yorktown!*" No Japanese commander from Yamamoto on down had dreamed that three American flattops would oppose their invasion of Midway. That one of them was the *Yorktown*, believed sunk at the Battle of the Coral Sea, must have added a chilling aspect to the news. Without hesitation Yamaguchi decided to send every available plane against the two undamaged carriers.

Down on the flight deck, the admiral shook hands with each of the pilots, with the words, *"Shikkari yatte koi"* (Hope for a good fight). A few moments later, at approximately 1330, ten torpedo bombers and six escorting fighters took to the air. In overall tactical command was Lt. Joichi Tomonaga. Tomonaga, whose left-wing gas tank had been damaged during the Midway raid that morning, knew he could carry only enough fuel for a one-way trip to the American fleet. Japanese survivors recall a general sense among the fliers and the men on the *Hiryu* that their attack would be suicidal. But no one seems to have hesitated.

Fewer than a hundred miles now separated the Japanese carrier from the nearest American one. In barely an hour, Tomonaga would be over his target.

HAD IT NOT BEEN FOR THE FORESIGHT OF THE *YORKTOWN*'S DAMAGE-CONTROL OFFICER, Comdr. Clarence E. Aldrich, who ordered all fuel lines drained and filled with carbon dioxide before the Japanese attack, the carrier would have suffered far more than it did. In the two hours since the noon dive-bomber attack, the repair crews on the *Yorktown* had worked a minor miracle. The big hole in the flight deck near frame 132 had been patched, the various fires extinguished, and the radar was back working. Most important, the undamaged boilers had been relit. At 1350 the engine room reported that it could make 20 knots or more. The breakdown flag was lowered from the signal bridge and replaced with the flag indicating 12 knots, then 16, then 18. Men on the watching escorts cheered the stubborn carrier that had come to life again.

But the *Yorktown* was no longer the flagship of the American battle fleet. The same black smoke that had poured into Vane Bennett's radar room had sent the admiral and his staff scurrying from the flag plot, or admiral's bridge, down onto the flight deck. Unable to maintain communications with his fleet, Fletcher quickly decided to move his flag to the cruiser *Astoria*, the flagship of the *Yorktown*'s escort. The *Yorktown* was without power and severely damaged, leaving the admiral little choice. When it came time to climb over the side to enter the *Astoria*'s whaleboat, Fletcher balked. "I'm too damn old for this sort of thing," he admitted, as he was lowered over the side.

By the time the admiral's staff had completed their transfer to the *Astoria*, Radio

(Left) Damage-control crews rush to repair a bomb hole in the flight deck. The *Yorktown*'s crews, under the leadership of the distant but respected Capt. Elliott Buckmaster (above), had the decks patched and the ship under way within two hours of the Japanese attack.

Electrician Bennett was back at his post in the radar room. This time, he left the door ajar. Capt. Elliott Buckmaster anticipated another attack at any minute. Soon Bennett's mind was completely focused on the radar scope in front of him.

LIEUTENANT TOMONAGA LED HIS TORPEDO BOMBERS STRAIGHT FOR THE *YORKTOWN*'S position. When the carrier came into view from a distance of about 30 miles, he saw that it was making good speed through the water and showed no obvious signs of damage. Not unnaturally, he assumed it was one of the unharmed American flattops. Tomonaga divided his force in half to attack simultaneously from port and starboard.

From his position in the observer/commander's seat, Petty Officer 1st Class

Taisuke Maruyama could see the enemy carrier and its ring of escorts. The Kates were armed with 800 kg Type 91 torpedoes, the same model they had used at Pearl Harbor. He and his group began their long glide toward the target. Almost immediately American fighters rose to meet them. Soon a Wildcat was on their tail.

"All I could think of at that moment was how we were going to get away from the Grumman," Maruyama remembers. "But our plane responded slowly because of the torpedo. Many bullets hit us. Two more Grummans came after us. Both the vertical and horizontal tail surfaces were riddled with bullet holes. They looked like honey

(Above) Lt. Joichi Tomonaga led the torpedo attack on the *Yorktown*, even though his damaged plane could no longer carry enough fuel for the return trip. (Right) A Japanese Kate torpedo plane rushes in to make its attack on the *Yorktown*.

combs. But still we kept flying. Then I glanced back and saw that our fuel tank had been hit. It's all over, I thought to myself. Then I saw the white fog leaking from the tank, indicating that the carbon dioxide was working to prevent a fire. We still had a chance. We began to descend to the attack."

The last fighter following Maruyama's plane veered off to avoid the *Yorktown*'s antiaircraft barrage. Thinking only of his target, Maruyama guided his aircraft to launch level. The American guns were lobbing shells just in front of his flight path, sending up great geysers of water. The pilot found, however, that he could predict the shot pattern and weave around it. Soon he was inside the range of the big guns and flying at an altitude of only 15 meters, beneath the antiaircraft fire.

"We dropped the torpedo at a distance of 300 meters, at a speed of 42 knots. The position and angle were perfect, but only because the carrier was moving so slowly, far less than 25 knots. We were now too close to the ship to bank away without catching our wingtip in the water, so we flew over the flight deck. I saw the faces of the men at the antiaircraft guns. Part of the flight deck was on fire."

Then Maruyama's Kate was beyond the ship, with flak bursting in its wake as it slowly gained altitude. Maybe he would make it after all.

Straining to make 20 knots, the *Yorktown* sends up a storm of flak as the torpedo planes attack.

AS THE *YORKTOWN*'S DAYTIME OFFICER OF THE DECK, LT. (JG.) JOHN GREENBACKER HAD THE JOB of conning the ship when things were quiet. Whenever enemy planes were sighted, Captain Buckmaster took over. This left Greenbacker, the youngest officer on the bridge, free to watch the action.

"The Japanese torpedo planes came through a furious crescendo of AA fire from both our own guns and those of the support ships," he recalled. "They seemed to keep coming in miraculously untouched. Their determination was impressive (and frightening), but equally impressive was the performance of our fighter aircraft, which were

barely able to take off at this speed, most of them unrefueled. They courageously banked sharply to the left immediately upon being airborne and flew directly down our own line of fire, making head-on passes against the incoming torpedo planes."

Commander Thach, who'd spent the first attack cooling his heels in his ready room, was one of the first in the air, flying a fresh Wildcat held in reserve. Close behind him was Lt. Bill Leonard, the young acting executive officer and Thach's second in command, who'd flown combat air patrol (CAP) that morning while Thach had escorted the torpedo planes to the enemy fleet. Leonard had fought at Coral Sea but this was his first chance of the day to tangle with the enemy.

He met his first adversary as it approached the ship on an almost reciprocal course. The Japanese plane presented an ideal target as it descended steadily preparatory to dropping its torpedo. The enemy pilot dropped his fish before Leonard could get him in his sights. The American pilot fired and saw the Kate crash into the water as he banked sharply to pick up a second target. "As I was looking over my shoulder," he recalls, "I saw this great upside-down Niagara" erupt from the side of the ship where the torpedo had struck. "There was no flame, no fire, no smoke, but the ship gently slowed to a stop. It hadn't yet taken on a list, but we knew that something terrible had happened because we'd seen that cascade of water."

From his perch on the catwalk, Bill Surgi found his attention riveted on one of the Japanese planes that approached from the port side. After it dropped its torpedo, it roared across the bow of the ship, leveling its wings for the flypast. Surgi could see the pilot and behind him an observer with a camera and, in the rear seat, the radio gunner. (Surgi had ridden in the third seat during his own training as a flight engineer.) Instead of shooting, however, the radioman was waving—at least that's what it looked like—or possibly shaking his fist. Was it a salute? An act of defiance? A shout of victory? Surgi didn't have much time to ponder these questions.

The young sailor could see the torpedo with its bright yellow nose glinting in the sunlight through the water, shining "like a brand-new nickel." Then an earthquake that shot right off the Richter scale bounced him up like a ball, crashing his steel hat against the catwalk grating above his head. Falling planks from a

A Japanese plane-launched torpedo hits the *Yorktown* near the end of the battle, sending a gusher of seawater skyward.

nearby painting stage—the kind that was hung over the ship's side for painting the hull—fell on his right arm, breaking it at the elbow.

The second torpedo detonated like a huge aftershock: "It picked the ship up, shook it, and set it back down again," according to Electrician's Mate 3rd Class Pete Newberg, who was part of Gordon Skinner's damage-control party. It certainly left Surgi's battle station a shambles. He and two other men were trapped beneath a tangle of wood and twisted metal. When he worked himself free, Surgi found his shipmate, Aviation Ordnance Man 3rd Class David Patterson, impaled through the thigh on a railing stanchion. He had to climb over Patterson in order to go for help.

By the time the last of the attackers either had been shot down or had turned for home, the *Yorktown*'s deck slanted so badly that its surviving fighters couldn't land. (Four had been shot down.) They headed for the *Enterprise*. Some, like Bill Leonard, landed just before their fuel ran out.

Two Japanese torpedoes had penetrated the port side of the *Yorktown*'s hull beneath the waterline, jamming the rudder, knocking out or cutting all power connections, and rupturing the port-side fuel tanks. "The hits could not have been better placed," recalled John Greenbacker. "The ship quickly listed to port about 20°. Further listing accumulated at a slower rate, but from the inclinometer on the bridge, it was apparent it was still slowly increasing. First 22°, then 23°, finally very slowly to 26°, where it hung. We could not be sure that it had gone as far as it would go. Up on the bridge, out in the open, there was no sense of panic."

ONLY FIVE KATES AND THREE ZEROS, HALF OF THE *HIRYU*'S SECOND ATTACKING FORCE, returned to their ship. (Lieutenant Tomonaga was almost certainly shot down by Jimmy Thach.) But the Japanese pilots could report that a second American carrier had been disabled. Even had the reports been true, Yamaguchi's situation was still very dire indeed.

His ship was as yet untouched by enemy attack, but his air force was a battle-scarred and battle-weary dreg. The dive-bomber attack had cost him 13 Vals and 3 Zeros, leaving him a grand total of 4 torpedo planes, 5 dive-bombers, and 6 fighters with which to do battle against at

(Above) Within minutes of being struck by two torpedoes, the *Yorktown* was listing heavily, transforming the flight deck into a perilous slope. (Below) The destroyer *Balch* stands by the crippled carrier during the late stages of abandonment. Hanging from the side are the lines that the *Yorktown*'s crew used to leave the ship.

least one fully armed American flattop, not to mention the forces remaining on Midway. Yet he unhesitatingly gave orders to prepare for a dusk attack. Unlike the Americans, the Japanese were highly skilled at night operations.

AS THE *YORKTOWN* SLOWED TO A STOP, THE MEN ON THE BRIDGE STOOD IN A KIND OF SHOCKED silence, according to Greenbacker. Comdr. Clarence E. Aldrich finally made his way to the bridge and with impressive calm pointed out to the captain that there was simply nothing he could do to take the list off the ship. "The captain paced up and down the starboard catwalk in agony for several minutes, saying he hated to give the order to abandon ship. He talked on in this vein for a moment as we all gaped at him mutely, and finally he said there was nothing else to do—we must abandon ship. And so the order was spread by word of mouth and sound-powered telephones throughout the ship." Buckmaster realized he could not risk the lives of some 2,300 officers and enlisted men if the *Yorktown* was in danger of capsizing.

The order to abandon ship came a little late for Pete Newberg, who seems to have been shaken right off the carrier during the torpedo attack. "The next thing I knew, I was in the water," he recalls. Soon he was covered with a thickening layer of bunker oil from a ruptured fuel tank. "I was wearing flash clothing and a life jacket on top of that, and I still had on my tin hat. All this gear made it terribly hard to swim."

After the torpedoes struck, Gordon Skinner had headed for the ship's high starboard side, which he did by crawling up the incline of the flight deck, using as handholds the metal strips for tying down airplanes. The climb so hurt his knees that he finally turned around and pushed himself upward on his butt. By the time Skinner reached the starboard rail, lines had already been thrown over the side and men were clambering down them, hand over hand. He worked his way to the fantail, where he figured the drop to the water would be less severe. There he found his boss, Chief Electrician's Mate Herbert Quarder, who had come out of retirement when the war started. Chief Quarder, who must have been all of 45, didn't have a life jacket. Skinner gave him his. Then he took off his shoes, placed them neatly alongside the others already lined up there, and went down one of the knotted ropes, hand over hand.

"A lot of people had rope burns," Skinner recalls, "but I didn't have that problem. When I got down to a point just above the water, I stopped climbing. It seems silly now, but I touched the water with one toe to see how warm it was before going in."

Like many *Yorktown* survivors, Bill Surgi has a vivid memory of the shoes lined up along the starboard rail. "I'm looking down the hangar deck, and I see the shoes, all lined up, believe it or not, with watches, billfolds, you name it. I'll never forget that sight." Because of his broken arm, Surgi slid down the slimy hull like a tobogganer, using his good hand to hold on to his steel hat. His life jacket, which he had forgotten to cinch, floated free as he splashed down, but he caught up with it. It made a lovely shelf for his broken arm as he began to paddle away from the ship with the other arm. (In Lieutenant Greenbacker's estimation, the *Yorktown's* abandonment was a disorganized mess. "Captain Buckmaster not only hated to order abandon ship, he had hated to practice it....")

Vane Bennett, bleeding from a head wound, was among the last to leave the ship, being one of those who toured belowdecks looking for wounded. He and about ten others made their way to the stern, where they waited for Captain Buckmaster to complete his final inspection in search of anyone left behind. Some climbed down one of the lines. Others, including Bennett, jumped the ten feet or so to the water.

Buckmaster was the last man overboard, believing he was the only person still alive on a sinking ship. Like a much younger man, he lowered himself hand over hand down one of the lines dangling from the fantail, then began to swim away. Nearby, a sailor shouted for help. This turned out to be William Fentress, a mess attendant, who clearly didn't know how to swim and was flailing about in the oily water. Buckmaster calmed Fentress down and kept his head above water until both of the men were rescued by the destroyer *Hammann*.

Act Five: The Knockout Blow

AT 1640, THE *KAGA*'S RANKING OFFICER FINALLY ORDERED THE SHIP ABANDONED. Comdr. Takahisa Amagai, an airman not a sailor, had assumed command after the American bomb wiped out the bridge. His firefighters could make no headway against the flames that continued to set off explosions, some of which blew men overboard. It was time to save all those he could.

Haruo Yoshino didn't hear the order "Abandon ship," but he could see others making their way to the high side where the destroyer *Hagikaze* was ready to pick up the crewmen who were already jumping overboard. "By the time I jumped, the destroyer had moved away" he recalls. "I jumped about seven or eight meters. I looked for something to hold on to and found some wood. There was nothing to do other than to wait. I thought we would be finished if the destroyer did not return.

"I think it was two or three hours later that the destroyer approached and dropped a raft. When the raft came by me, I told the crew that I could swim, but they told me to climb on board. I did. The raft took me to the *Hagikaze*.

"On board the destroyer, I met a relative. This was a most embarrassing moment. I was a defeated warrior. He helped me dry my wet clothes. I was deeply embarrassed to appear in such a condition in front of a relative. I worried that he would tell everybody about it when he returned home."

Yuji Akamatsu's escape from the *Kaga* was considerably more adventurous than Yoshino's. Drops from a leaking water tank brought him back to consciousness in the now deserted ready room. His head was still bleeding as he made his way up to the hangar deck. "The iron plate was burning," he remembers. "The rubber soles of my shoes melted and I could barely move. The fires drove me up onto the flight deck, where the black smoke made it almost impossible to breathe.

"I went to the ship's side and looked over. It was so high that I was scared to jump. The fire was coming closer. I had to do something. I raced down the deck to the other side, closed my eyes, and jumped. I had a life jacket on, so I floated to the surface fairly quickly."

Those still on the ship threw over the side wooden boxes, empty bomb cartons, and anything that would float. These became life buoys for those without life jackets and for the wounded. Akamatsu's squadron leader floated nearby, badly burned. "We gathered the boxes and hoisted the senior officer on top of them. There were explosions all around us, and I was afraid of being hit by shrapnel. I wanted to swim as far away from the *Kaga* as I could, but I couldn't desert my squadron leader. We all cooperated to keep him on top of the boxes as we swam alongside them. It was very difficult but we managed somehow."

After an hour, maybe more, in the oily waters, Akamatsu was picked up by a destroyer, almost certainly the *Hagikaze*. The waves were rising and the more badly wounded couldn't climb the lines thrown over the side of the ship. "Many of my shipmates were left in the water. Some died naturally, some commited suicide, shouting 'Long live the emperor!'

"On board the destroyer there was absolute silence. We had been saved, but we felt no sense of relief. We were dead tired, and we didn't have the strength to speak."

ADMIRAL FLETCHER HAD OBSERVED THE SECOND ATTACK ON THE *YORKTOWN* FROM ON BOARD the *Astoria*. Unlike Admiral Nagumo, however, who stubbornly attempted to exercise full command of the Japanese forces from the cruiser *Nagara*, Fletcher quickly elected to relinquish his position. At the beginning of the battle, he had ceded a greater degree of independence to Spruance than any of the Japanese admirals under Nagumo had enjoyed. Now he sent a message to the *Enterprise*, placing the direction of the last phase of the battle in his subordinate's capable hands. Spruance, as he had done throughout the day, quickly seized the initiative.

About the time the *Hiryu*'s second attack hit the *Yorktown*, the scouting force that Fletcher had dispatched before the first Japanese attack discovered the *Hiryu*—the remaining Japanese aircraft carrier with its powerful escort of battleships, cruisers, and destroyers. At 1530, while the *Yorktown* was being abandoned, the *Enterprise* had launched 25 dive-bombers, including 14 formerly from the *Yorktown*, against the enemy. Spruance held back all his fighters in case of another Japanese attack. The *Hornet* didn't start launching until almost half an hour after the *Enterprise*, about the time the *Enterprise* group headed off for the *Hiryu*. (Spruance's staff had forgotten to relay the order.) Yet again, disorganization and poor communication ruined chances of a coordinated attack—at least one that was planned in advance.

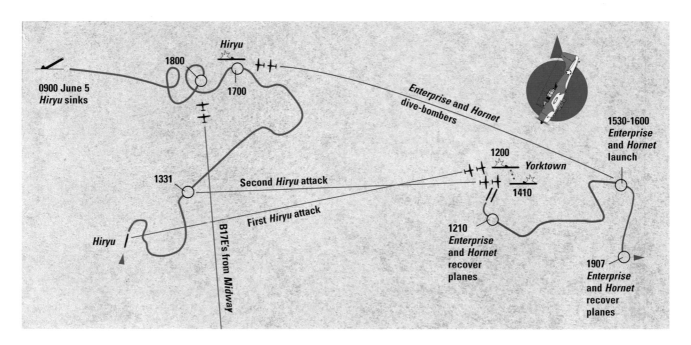

0900 June 5
Hiryu sinks

1800

Hiryu
1700

Enterprise and Hornet dive-bombers

1530-1600
Enterprise
and *Hornet*
launch

1331

Second Hiryu attack

1200 *Yorktown*

1410

Hiryu

First Hiryu attack

B17E's from Midway

1210
Enterprise
and *Hornet*
recover
planes

1907
Enterprise
and *Hornet*
recover
planes

On the afternoon of June 4, while the *Yorktown* was being abandoned, American bombers from the *Enterprise* found and severely damaged the *Hiryu*.

By 1658, not long after the last of the *Hiryu*'s planes had been recovered from their torpedo attack, the bombers from the *Enterprise* arrived over Admiral Nagumo's last aircraft carrier and prepared to dive. With Wade McClusky recuperating from wounds in the *Enterprise*'s sick bay, the senior remaining squadron commander, Lt. Earl Gallaher, was making the decisions. Inexplicably he chose to divide his force, directing the ten bombers originally from the *Yorktown* to attack one of the escorting battleships, while he led the remaining 14 against the lone carrier. When the *Hiryu* appeared to be successfully dodging this attack, one of the two groups aiming for the battleship abruptly shifted targets, turning on the carrier. The sudden course change forced the second of Gallaher's two squadrons to maneuver desperately to avoid midair collisions, in the process making themselves targets for the ten Zeros that had risen to meet them.

If the method was haphazard, the result was decisive. One of the planes in Gallaher's first group slammed a bomb into the *Hiryu*'s forward elevator; it passed through the flight deck and blew up, with devastating consequences. Three more bombs are believed to have hit the ship, which became, in *Yorktown* historian Robert Cressman's words, "a floating cauldron of exploding gasoline and ordnance."

Yamaguchi's valiant Zeros buzzed the retreating Americans, but they lost only three planes in the attack, which had left the Japanese pilots with no place to land. Though the *Hiryu* was still under way, her flight deck was in flames. With this knockout blow, the Japanese mobile force became a hollow shell, a ring of escorts with nothing to escort. (The *Hornet*'s bombers showed up 15 minutes later, attacked the burning carrier's escort against no aerial opposition but failed to score a single hit.) For all practical purposes, the Battle of Midway seemed to be over, the result a stunning American victory.

Defeat proved too much for Rear Adm. Tamon Yamaguchi, who concluded that his only honorable exit from the *Hiryu* was the traditional one for a Japanese samurai—*hara-kiri*. He would stay with his ship until long after sunset, hoping against hope that it could be saved. Early on the morning of June 5, his officers stood with him on the one corner of the flight deck not yet consumed by flames. To a man they offered to stay with the admiral, but he ordered them all to leave. They were young; Japan needed them. No one saw Yamaguchi's final moments, but his most devoted officer, Lt. Comdr. Takeo Kyuma, who had served with him longer than any of the others, provided this sterling epitaph: "I had admired him for a long time and still believe he was the greatest man I have ever met in my whole life."

But on the late afternoon of June 4, total defeat for Japan was not yet certain. Admiral Yamamoto's main force, including three battleships and one light aircraft carrier which had lurked powerfully to the rear of the action, was already charging forward. Yamamoto had diverted the Japanese force moving toward the Aleutians, which meant that its two attack carriers and their escorts were already sailing south toward Midway. The American admirals could not yet count the enemy out. The Japanese still hoped to lure them into a battle that would even the score.

With the *Hiryu* on fire (above and below), her ranking officer ordered the ship abandoned. Some of her survivors (opposite) who had escaped in a longboat were later picked up by the Americans.

ACCORDING TO COMDR. MITSUO FUCHIDA, ADMIRAL NAGUMO SEEMED unwilling to accept reality, even after he watched the *Hiryu* engulfed in flames. To almost every member of Nagumo's staff aboard the light cruiser *Nagara*, however, "the grim situation was painfully clear," wrote Fuchida. "Our air strength was wiped out. The enemy still had at least one carrier intact, we had failed to render the Midway airfields ineffective, and some of our ships were still within striking range of planes based there. With command of the air firmly in enemy hands, the outcome of the battle was a foregone conclusion." Yet no one was willing to counsel withdrawal, while a lone staff officer, Comdr. Tamotsu Oishi, feverishly hatched plans for a night attack by surface ships. To Fuchida, such a notion seemed nothing less than foolhardy. Even assuming the Americans could be engaged and all their carriers sunk—an outrageously improbable scenario—the Japanese would still be in range of Midway-based aircraft the following morning. Only when Nagumo received the following discouraging report from one of his few remaining scout planes did he finally order a withdrawal to the northwest: "At 1713 this ship's No. 2 plane sighted 4 enemy carriers, 6 cruisers, and 15 destroyers at a point 30 miles east of the burning carrier. The enemy force is proceeding westward." It was only the latest in the confusing series of reports on the number of American carriers that had added to Nagumo's command confusion.

The sun that sank on Admiral Nagumo's last hopes of evening the score also sank on three of his four helpless aircraft carriers. The *Soryu* had sunk at 1915. The *Akagi* would go next morning, seen off by Japanese torpedos. Yuji Akamatsu watched the *Kaga*'s final moments from the deck of the *Hagikaze*, which stood about 3,000 yards from the smoldering ship. Eight hundred of his shipmates had died on what was

now a derelict hulk, but for hours it had refused to go down. Finally the other destroyer, the *Maikaze*, fired a single torpedo, hitting the carrier amidships and appearing to break it in two. "I thought of my mother first," remembers Akamatsu, "and then the emperor. Then I thought, I want to die, too."

Haruo Yoshino also watched from the *Hagikaze*: "About sundown, everyone was ordered up on deck. It was miserable, shameful. The splendid *Kaga* that looked so dignified just that morning.... There is no way to express it with words. It gave me a taste of the bitterness of war, the bitterness of defeat. Our destroyer moved in and fired a single torpedo. With the setting sun behind us and the sinking ship to the east, it was almost like a shadow painting. I felt nothing but misery."

Chapter Five

Searching for Ghosts

Saturday, May 9, 1998

THIS MORNING, AS WE SETTLED INTO THE FIRST FULL DAY OF HUNTING for the Japanese aircraft carriers *Kaga* and *Akagi*, I hit a wall. A mental one. I began to really doubt that we were ever going to find even a rusty depth charge. During the course of every expedition there seems to come a time when the morale of the team gets very low. With our search for the *Titanic*, the gloom didn't set in until the 11th hour. With the *Bismarck*, it arrived the second year when, with time almost gone, we still hadn't found the German battleship. With Midway, the negative thoughts have turned up early—a product of the mounting number of technical foul-ups and the larger uncertainties surrounding this particular challenge. Now, after almost ten days at sea, people are keeping more to themselves. The two Japanese veterans seem especially self-contained, which I guess is not surprising. I often see them standing at the bow just staring at the sea, not talking much. I wonder what they're thinking, what they're remembering.

The U.S. Navy team, which has been working around the clock to fix the wounded ATV, is getting understandably cranky, and for the most part I stay out of their way so as not to put too much pressure on them. If I want a report on their progress, I generally get it through Dave Mindell or Jay Minkin. Since Jay is at loose ends unless the ATV is in the water, he has been spending a lot of time helping out with repairs. He seems to be getting along well with the Navy techies. Peter Schnall, who's supposed to be making a great documentary about our expedition, is looking more and more worried: If we don't get the ATV fixed, he doesn't have a movie. Even if we get the ATV fixed, we won't have a movie unless we find something—anything.

(Opposite) Two Navy crewman ease out cable during an ATV launch. Unfortunately, for most of the time we were searching for the Japanese carriers, the ATV stayed on deck, as Navy technicians worked frantically to get it operational.

I usually don't let these kinds of doubts get to me. My job is to keep up the morale, not contribute to the malaise. The truth is, however, that I am as worried as I have ever been.

I've even started to obsess about the black-footed albatrosses that have been following our ship since we left land. At least the birds are one thing we have in common with 1942. Bill Surgi says an albatross followed the *Yorktown* wherever it went in the Pacific. As a scientist I'm not supposed to be superstitious, but I have spent too much of my life at sea to be completely immune. (As long as we don't shoot one, like the Ancient Mariner, maybe everything will be all right.)

The best antidote for these low moods is work. After break-fast this morning, Chuck Haberlein and I went over once again all the information we have about the Japanese carriers. When the two Japanese veterans came on board, they presented me with a set of positions for the four aircraft carriers that sank at the Battle of Midway. But these positions don't add anything to the data we have, since Admiral Nagumo's action report was translated into English not long after the war was over. Nagumo's fixes agree quite closely with the ones published by Mitsuo Fuchida in his book *Midway: The Battle That Doomed Japan*. Chuck Haberlein is hopeful that Japanese navigation was better than American, which he takes to be one of the possible lessons from the ships we found a few years ago at Guadalcanal. My experience hunting for the *Bismarck* suggests that the best of navigators falter in the heat of battle. All in all, I think we will be incredibly lucky if the Japanese aircraft carriers are within ten miles of the positions we have been given.

(Top) I discuss our strategy for finding the *Kaga* with Mr. Yoshino and Mr. Akamatsu as the search continues. (Above) Yuji Akamatsu contemplates an enlarged schematic of his ship, the *Kaga*.

Three of the four carriers—the *Soryu*, the *Akagi*, and the *Kaga*—are officially close enough together that we could realistically search for all three. But the *Soryu* supposedly blew up before it sank. If it's in more than a few big pieces, our sonar almost certainly won't see it. I'm a lot more optimistic about the other two wrecks. According to Admiral Nagumo's official report of the battle, the *Kaga* sank after "two great explosions," implying that the ship went down in several pieces. But Haruo Yoshino and Yuji Akamatsu, who both saw the *Kaga*'s final moments, swear they saw their ship sink in one piece after it was deliberately scuttled by a torpedo fired from the *Maikaze*. Naturally we're hoping the *Kaga* is in good shape. It's the ship I want to find most of all.

Our search quadrant places the *Kaga* and *Akagi* positions inside a rectangle about 25 nautical miles by 10 nautical miles, or 250 square miles—huge in deep-ocean terms. It means an awful lot of ground for *MR-1* to cover, and until a few days ago I had no idea what sort of landscape we would be flying over. We began the expedition with nothing like the detailed topographical survey of the Japanese battlefield that the Navy had created for the *Yorktown* search area. I was moaning about this problem to Bruce Appelgate, whose team from the University of Hawaii has performed so splendidly. Bruce looked at me and asked if I had considered a satellite topographical map. It turns out that, using gravity readings, a satellite can make a picture of the ocean floor that is almost as detailed as the Navy map we used for the *Yorktown*. A few hours later, Bruce delivered a beautiful color chart that he had downloaded from our ship-

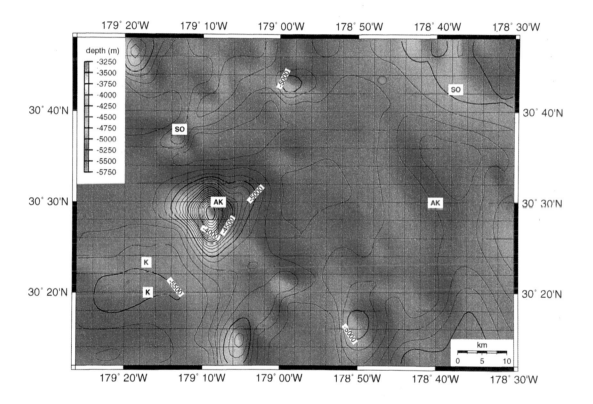

On our colorful satellite topographical chart of the Japanese search area, we pasted on name tags to mark the various reported sinking locations for the three Japanese carriers we thought we had a real chance of finding: SO = *Soryu;* AK = *Akagi;* K = *Kaga*.

board Internet. Remarkable. Soon we will be using satellites to hunt for shipwrecks.

This satellite chart has revealed a terrain remarkably similar to the *Yorktown* search area—plains to the south, mountains to the north. The *Kaga* position is the more southerly of the two. It is located in what looks like a fairly even abyssal plain—perfect for *MR-1*. The *Akagi* lies more to the north, in the volcanic foothills. Of course our whole search strategy assumes the ships are in the vicinity that Nagumo and Fuchida said they were. Which, given the haze of battle, is assuming a lot.

In other words, this morning I was still fairly worried when I looked into the wet lab to check on how the sonar survey was going. (At least *MR-1* has worked like a dream—so far.) Bruce Appelgate and I examined the printout from the real-time sonar monitor. At the slow *ping* rate, this inches out of its printer at a frustratingly slow pace. We noted several possible targets. But only more passes and more computer analysis will determine whether any of these blips is worth visiting.

Next door in the War Room, Cathy Offinger was finishing off the night shift. Cathy and I joke around constantly—we've known each other so long and have such respect for each other that we are really more like brother and sister than colleagues. Her participation in this expedition gives me a solid sense of security.

Cathy showed me the plot of the *Laney*'s course during the night. Standing navigation watch during a sonar search is pretty basic. The main job is double-checking our course and position. Cathy had noted this every half hour in a written log. Then, by comparing that log with the officially recorded course, we can be sure the *Laney* has actually covered the ground we think it has and that there are no gaps in our coverage. Mowing the lawn at sea is very different from cutting real grass at home. For one thing, the lawn mower's handle is three miles long. For another, the swath we cut has that big gap in the middle—*MR-1*'s blind spot. Currents and winds screw up the nice straight lines you've drawn on the chart. A shipwreck can easily get lost in the cracks.

Cathy certainly didn't need any help from me. I decided to wander out on the stern to see how the Navy crew was coming with repairs to the ATV. I figured they wouldn't mind a brief visit from the customer. I'm getting good at timing my dash across the open deck. Today I hardly got a splash. I paused for a moment once I had reached the raised afterdeck to look at the sea and the sky—the same sea and sky as 56 years ago. There was a light breeze blowing, and crying seabirds wheeled overhead. Albatrosses, probably. At least none of those damn birds was hanging around the ATV on the stern.

I found Chief Swarm and several of his men surrounded by pieces of the vehicle. One was consulting a circuitry diagram. Another was working on the hydraulic motor. I offered my standard greeting: "Hey, howya doin'?"

"We should have her ready to go back into the water tomorrow," the chief assured me.

I stayed for a few minutes of conversation. But the last thing these young sailors needed was me breathing down their necks. They knew their reputation was on the line.

Back in the War Room, another long gray strip of paper, representing a single sonar swath across our search area, lay on the chart. In a few moments I had it in place. I stared at the sonar picture beginning to take shape on my light table. The minutes passed, and the room began to recede from my consciousness as I began to visualize the landscape far below. To an unpracticed eye, the printout resembles a blur of soft shadows embedded in a background of gray fog. But I have been staring at these things since I was a grad student researching my dissertation on plate tectonic activity on the seafloor off New England. First and last, I am a geologist. And the sonar plot was showing me a picture as beautiful as the sight from a plane flying over the Rockies on a cloudless day.

It's hard to explain, but sometimes I feel as though I can actually *see* the bottom—not up close but with an airplane's-eye view from an altitude of 17,000 feet, seeing the plains, the great rivers of lava, and their many tributaries. To my geologist's eye nature has sculpted all of these elements together in a beautiful and wonderfully logical way. Soon I was visualizing how those volcanoes were formed and how volcanic flows had run down their steep slopes. It was an exhilarating feeling. After a few days of flying

In our darkened War Room, Bruce Appelgate and I ponder the latest sonar information collected.

around like this, I will really know the territory where my targets lie.

I will also know if there is anything resembling a ship down there—or a landslide in the thick deposit of sediment covering the volcanoes. If we find evidence like that, we can follow it to the ship—the way we did with *Bismarck*.

Sunday, May 10

THERE'S NOTHING MUCH TO REPORT TODAY—EXCEPT THAT THE FOOD ON BOARD ISN'T getting any better. It always deteriorates after a week or more away from port. The sonar survey of the Japanese search area will be completed tomorrow. We have already identified several promising targets, but most of those will disappear once we have covered them from more than one direction. Maybe one of them is the *Kaga*. Or the *Akagi*. On the even better news front, the Navy claims it will have the ATV up and running by midnight, which means we may actually have a vehicle to send down to look at any targets that measure up. I certainly hope they're right. I'll believe it when I see it.

There is no sign that the suspense is getting to our friends from Japan. But Bill Surgi is up to something. I just know it. He's spending an inordinate amount of time in the ship's workshop. Bill is quite a character—never idle and always full of stories. Harry Ferrier, on the other hand, seems to be drawing into himself. It's not surprising. I gather one of his best friends died not long before he left home, and his wife has

recently been ill. Now he's sailing around the same piece of ocean where he lost all his buddies so many years ago. It can't be easy for him.

AFTER SUPPER, PETER SCHNALL AND I HAD ONE OF OUR RARE DISAGREEMENTS. WE HAVE KNOWN each other a long time. He was with me on our very first JASON expedition, when we discovered a Roman wreck off Sicily, and on both our *Bismarck* expeditions—the first year when we hunted but found nothing, and the second year when we finally found the ship. He has also been on several trips since then, so we have developed a good working relationship. But that doesn't mean we always see things the same way.

The sun was getting low in the sky as we strolled out onto the bow. This is really the one place on the ship where you can have a private conversation or be by yourself. Space is so limited that most of the team is sleeping four to a cabin.

I've seen quite a few tropical sunsets, but I never get tired of them. This one was a stunner: billowing clouds brushed with crimson, deep purple, and orange. Peter and I talked about our wives and kids, as we often do.

Then I got around to the point.

"As soon as we've finished the survey, I think we should pull up stakes and head back to the *Yorktown*," I told him. "Until I know for sure we've got one ship, I don't want to spend any more time looking for the others."

"I can't agree, Bob," Peter shot back. "The Japanese are an important part of our story. In a few more days they'll be gone. It's really important that we find the *Kaga*."

When Peter and I disagree, we don't shout or get angry. We don't even raise our voices. But he wasn't about to go along with me, either. As he quite correctly pointed out, we would not only be losing our Japanese veterans in a few days, we would also be losing our sonar team. Once *MR-1* was out of the water for good, we could wave good-bye to any chance of finding the Japanese carriers.

"But what if our first target isn't the *Yorktown*?" I countered.

"Then we don't have a movie. But it's a chance I've got to take."

Filmmaker Peter Schnall (above) and with his crew (opposite and below), filming the ATV's descent.

In the end I relented. After all, without National Geographic's support we wouldn't have an expedition. Peter depends on me; I depend on him. It just goes to show how complicated this explorer business has become in the age of mass media. We serve many masters now—science, history, and entertainment. The balancing act between them is always difficult, but the way I look at it, the entertainment aspect is justified only if it serves the science and the history. And there's no question that Peter's documentary will bring the story of Midway to many people who know little or nothing about it now.

Tonight I'm going to hit the sack early. Tomorrow we may actually get to see a Japanese aircraft carrier that no one has looked at for 56 years. If I were like General Patton, I'd get down on my knees and pray for the health of our television vehicle.

Monday, May 11

MAYBE CHUCK HABERLEIN IS RIGHT AND THE ATV IS JINXED. THOSE BLACK-FOOTED albatrosses landed next to the vehicle as soon as it was winched over the side and down to the water. As usual, they took off just before it sank beneath the surface. A few minutes later one of its hydraulic pumps failed, which drained 60 percent of the vehicle's propulsive power. Then we discovered the altimeter wasn't working at all. With only 40 percent power, the thing took eight long hours to get to the bottom. Once it was there, the Navy couldn't move it forward at all. So we found ourselves in the absurd position of towing our "advanced" vehicle backward toward the target.

Oh, yes, the target. This morning we finally had enough sonar coverage to eliminate all but two contacts inside our designated search area. Both seemed solid possibilities. As far as Bruce Appelgate and Karen Sender are concerned, both of them pass the aircraft carrier test: They are the right size and shape and look the same from every angle. Only one of them exhibits a similar vertical relief when we pass over it with the depth sounder, but that may simply mean the ship is more deeply buried. (Karen has confessed, however, that her gut instinct isn't giving her the same positive reading as it did on the *Yorktown* target.) Encouragingly, the two positions corresponded roughly to the official positions for the *Kaga* and the *Akagi*. We decided to go for the *Kaga* first, since that is Haruo and Yuji's ship.

A briefing on the fantail for the ATV team before our descent on the *Kaga* target. We never did get the ATV working completely to our satisfaction during this phase of our search.

As we approached bottom depth, just about everyone who wasn't sleeping was glued to a video screen. Peter Schnall and his crew were with us in the control room, ready to film our reaction at our first sight of the *Kaga*. Since there was no room for Chuck Haberlein in the cramped control space, he stood in the hangar a few yards away, armed with Don Montgomery's models of the Japanese carriers, various drawings, and reference material. Our four veterans and just about everybody else had jammed into the wet lab where we have set up a video theater—a television monitor hooked up to the video coming from the bottom.

As the vehicle got close to the bottom, my heart began to sink. Its sonar was picking up only soft targets ahead of it, not sending back the hard *pings* that would indicate the hull of a ship. Nonetheless we towed the vehicle backward over the site we had identified.

But our "*Kaga*" turned out to be a shallow ridge, nothing more. To make matters worse, our translator, Junko Taguchi, somehow misunderstood what was going on and during our final approach told Haruo and Yuji that we had found the *Kaga*. So I guess their disappointment at not seeing their old ship was even greater. What a mess.

A big debate followed about what to do next. It's the kind of discussion that could only happen when your technology is functioning at half steam. The dilemma: Do we pull the ATV out and transit the 7.5 miles north to the *Akagi* site at top speed, or keep it down there and head north at a snail's pace? At a maximum speed of one knot, we calculate that it will take 10 to 12 hours to drag the vehicle up there. But recovery, transit, and relaunch will take about the same time. Since it is down there and working—more or less—we decide to leave it be.

Dave Mindell and I have both left instructions that we want to be wakened around 0430, when we should be getting close to the *Akagi*.

Tuesday, May 12

WELL, WE GOT TO THE POSSIBLE *AKAGI* SITE SOONER THAN EXPECTED. ABOUT AN HOUR after I had passed out in my bunk, Cathy came and woke me up. Feeling extremely groggy, I threw on some coveralls over my pajamas and stumbled down to the van. Dave was already there. We were both really annoyed to hear that during transit the vehicle had kited to a much higher altitude and that it would take several hours for it to sink back to the bottom—thanks to its weakened propulsion. There was no chance of sleeping now, so we went back to the War Room and waited while the ATV descended at about 15 feet a minute.

By 0600, the team was on discovery alert: Chuck was at the ready with his mounds of reference for helping us identify pieces of the ship; the veterans were sitting in the front row of our little video theater; Peter was filming in the van.

As the ATV approached the bottom, its sonar began to pick up scattered targets. A debris field! Then the main event—the target that was our last chance at seeing a Japanese carrier—came in loud and clear. In my mind's eye I was already cruising along the *Akagi*'s flight deck, examining the bomb damage that had driven Admiral Nagumo from his bridge.

Then the outline of a scalloped rock outcrop came into video view. So much for our chances of finding a Japanese shipwreck. The target proved to be a lovely piece of volcanic geology.

What a huge letdown. It's still early morning, but time loses meaning out here. I decided to get some sleep.

I DREAMED ABOUT DIVING AIRPLANES AND BURNING SHIPS AND WOKE UP SWEATING. WHEN I went out on deck to get some air, Haruo and Yuji were once again standing quietly at the bow rail. I knew they were planning a memorial ceremony for this afternoon.

It is hard to imagine what it must have been like for them, and for the several thousand other Japanese sailors—many badly burned or wounded by shrapnel—crowded onto those tiny destroyers through the long night after the battle. Like the men who had left most of their belongings on the abandoned *Yorktown*, they huddled on the destroyer decks with little or no cover. Those who had removed all or most of their clothes so they could swim more easily were lucky if they had a blanket. The worst death toll was from the *Soryu*, which had sunk first. The *Kaga* went down near sunset. The *Akagi* was scuttled near dawn. Thus when the sun rose, it rose on only one of the four great aircraft carriers, the *Hiryu*, which sank at 0900.

In some ways the worst part of the battle for Yuji, Haruo, and their comrades was what happened after they returned to Japan. The government was so afraid that news of the defeat would leak out to the Japanese people that it interned the sailors in military camps behind barbed wire fences, just as if they were prisoners of war.

Haruo Yoshino reads a Shinto prayer during the memorial ceremony he conducted at sea before we left the area where the *Kaga* sank. Standing beyond him along the rail are Yuji Akamatsu, Harry Ferrier, Bill Surgi, and me.

(Admittedly it was September 1942 before America publicly acknowledged the loss of the *Yorktown*.) Of course the news leaked out anyway.

Eventually the veterans of Midway returned to their military jobs. Both Yuji and Haruo were assigned to the carrier *Shokaku*, but they never again entered into combat with confidence in victory. By the end of the war, most of the men they had trained with had died.

WE GATHERED AT THE BOW. AT 1500 THE *LANEY* CAME TO ALL STOP. HARUO AND YUJI HAD prepared a Shinto ritual, which they read in Japanese. Harry Ferrier and Bill Surgi stood with them. At the end of the Japanese formalities, the two men scattered lotus blossoms on the surface and then anointed the ocean with water from Mount Fuji and specially blessed sake (rice wine).

Here's a translation of part of what Haruo said: "Today, America and Japan are working together to bring about world peace. We believe that the innumerable spirits who sacrificed their lives for their country should be forever honored for their distinguished service. We are honored to have fought alongside you in battle. Veterans from both countries have overcome past animosities and have pledged a renewed peace.

"Spirits, please rest in peace."

At the end of the ceremony, both Bill and Harry saluted, a lovely gesture that seemed a tribute to both their fallen comrades and their former adversaries. Then Bill presented his surprise. He had created facsimiles of a *Hiryu* memorial medallion struck for a reunion of the carrier's crew he had attended in Japan. (It was at this reunion that he'd met the Japanese radio gunner who had waved at him during the Japanese torpedo plane attack on the *Yorktown* on the afternoon of June 4. The man reported that he wasn't shaking his fist in a defiant gesture but expressing his relief at still being alive.) Using the original medal as a template, Bill had carefully made impressions with aluminum foil, then mounted each facsimile in a small handmade box with a Plexiglas lid. He presented one of these to each of the veterans and one to me. It was really a lovely touch and made the whole ceremony even more moving.

But I don't think the medallions were what got to Harry. Clearly the ceremony affected him deeply. It had momentarily dropped him back into the middle of the battle, back where his friends had died.

"I was thinking, as Haruo and Yuji were paying homage to their shipmates," he told Peter while the cameras rolled, "that I lost 45 shipmates at this very spot. Except for Bert Earnest and me, my whole squadron died. So this is a very solemn spot for me as well as for them. I hadn't thought about it too much until now. It brings back some pretty terrible memories.

"You know, you don't think about how you're going to react sometimes to a situation. Then the emotions come back and they flow. And it's pretty hard to stop them."

Wednesday, May 13

WE ARRIVED BACK AT MIDWAY AT 0600 AND SAID GOOD-BYE TO OUR NEW JAPANESE friends and to Harry Ferrier, who has decided to head for home. I completely understand; he's had his catharsis, and now he's just incredibly homesick. And by leaving now, he will get back in time to attend his friend's memorial. Dave Mindell, who had signed on for only the first half of the cruise, is also going back. He has to return to MIT to finish teaching for the semester. He is pretty disappointed not to have seen a shipwreck, but I have promised him that I will bring him back some nice pictures of the *Yorktown*. I hope I'm not just kidding myself.

It's hard to say how long we will be stuck here on shore—longer than I would like, anyway—while we wait for the new lights and pressure spheres that we have managed to beg and borrow to be installed on the ATV. But right now I just want to sleep. For about 24 hours straight.

May I wake up feeling more confident than I do now. The *Yorktown* target, which seemed so solid only a few days ago, no longer looks like such a sure thing. Not after two strong sonar targets that seemed to have the characteristics of the Japanese ships we were looking for turned out to be hunks of geology. I don't even want to think about the consequences if we strike out a third time. I don't like the taste of defeat, and I don't like letting people down.

Chapter Six
Yorktown's Farewell

June 5–7, 1942

THE DESTROYERS OF THE *YORKTOWN'S* ESCORT SAILED THROUGH THE NIGHT OF JUNE 4–5, 1942, their decks packed with the carrier's crewmen. Despite attempts to distribute the rescued evenly among them, some destroyers were dangerously top-heavy and in peril of capsizing, especially the *Benham*, which had rescued more than 700 men. In all, 2,270 men were rescued out of the roughly 2,300 on board.

"I spent the night under the wardroom table," remembers Bill Surgi, who was among those on the *Benham*. "I was one of the walking wounded. I didn't lie down, and I don't think I slept much, if at all. But I was a lot better off than the guys outside, lying on the steel decking. The doctors were using the

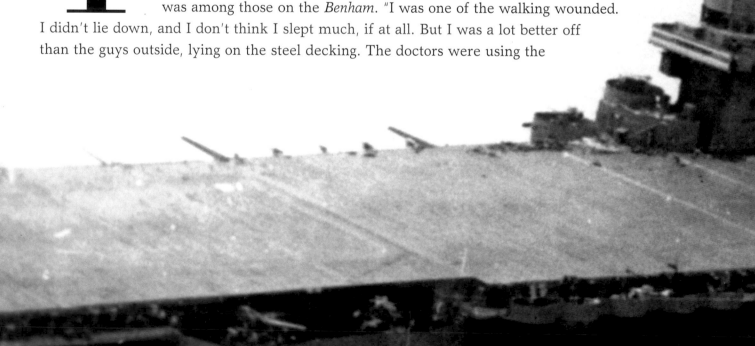

wardroom table to tend to the wounded. Some of them were pretty badly off."

Bill Surgi passed the night with an empty stomach, but not for want of food. In the ocean for three or four hours before being rescued, all the while resting his broken arm on his life-jacket pillow, he had swallowed a great deal of salt water and bunker oil. Once on board the *Benham*, he thirstily downed the warm tomato soup being distributed to the rescued. It tasted wonderful. But a few minutes later, he vomited it back up.

It was a "helluva miserable night," Pete Newberg remembers. He spent the hours till dawn with two shipmates from his hometown of Willmar, Minnesota, huddled between two of *Benham*'s torpedo tubes. In one of those improbable coincidences of war, the three, who hailed from different divisions and different parts of the ship, had found themselves together on the same life raft. In the warm water, Newberg had taken off all his clothes to make swimming easier. His two friends weren't much better off. Now the combination of the chill night air and the heat from the boiler room directly below had him by turns sweating and shivering. When word was passed that there was hot soup available in the galley, one of his friends brought some back in his steel battle helmet. Tomato soup had never tasted so good.

First light on June 5 found the abandoned *Yorktown* listing badly but still afloat. In this photo, shot the previous afternoon, two Wildcats can be seen on her empty flight deck, which shows remarkably little evidence of her recent battle.

Many of the 720 *Yorktown* survivors taken aboard by the *Benham* crowd the destroyer's decks as it pulls alongside the cruiser *Portland*. The listing *Yorktown* can be seen in the distance.

The officers had more to do than the enlisted men—even junior officers—as Lt. (jg.) John Greenbacker can attest: "As ship's secretary, I worked late into the night with my yeoman in the ship's office making out muster lists of all the refugees we had on board. There, during the course of the evening, someone returned to me the binoculars, now ruined by saltwater, and the pistol which I had left in the life raft." Exhausted, he finally bedded down for the night in the ship's wardroom.

Greenbacker was feeling rather guilty about having left the bridge without throwing overboard the cryptographic publications and coding equipment. Not that the Japanese seemed likely to show up before the *Yorktown* sank—but if they did, they would find on board a priceless trove of secret information. As ship's secretary, he had the job of destroying this classified material, and he had failed to do it in the confusion and anxiety of the abandonment.

Captain Buckmaster must have passed an uneasy night on board the *Astoria*, Admiral Fletcher's flagship of necessity, to which he had transferred after being rescued by the *Hammann*. Fletcher does not seem to have questioned Buckmaster's decision to order the *Yorktown* abandoned, but her captain undoubtedly wondered if he'd left his ship too soon. What could/should he have done differently? Late the previous afternoon, when the *Yorktown*'s escort departed, the carrier was still afloat and seemed to have stabilized at a 23° list. (One of the escorting destroyers, the *Hughes*, remained behind to keep watch and to sink her if necessary.) If she was in the same condition at daybreak, perhaps a salvage effort could be mounted.

Despite the damage to the *Yorktown*, Admiral Fletcher had every reason to be satisfied with American fortunes. He had gone into the battle judging it a "nip-and-tuck proposition." Before noon, when his planes put the three Japanese flattops out of action, he had felt "an indescribably wonderful feeling . . . a tremendous relief." By the time the sun had set, he was reasonably sure the American side had come out on top. His decision to cede tactical command of his two remaining carriers to his junior had paid off handsomely. Even though he had every right to board the *Hornet* and assume overall command, he would not presume to do so. Spruance had performed admirably during the battle. Fletcher saw no reason to fold a winning hand.

Armchair strategists later accused Admiral Spruance of timidity for failing to pursue the Japanese during the night of June 4–5, arguing he could have sunk more enemy ships the following morning. But Spruance, whom Midway authority Gordon Prange has aptly called "the admiral's admiral," knew better. He could not yet be sure all the enemy carriers had been put out of action. He may have been unaware of Yamamoto's powerful Main Force charging up from Nagumo's rear, but he knew the Japanese could potentially bring other ships, including other aircraft carriers, into play. And he wanted above all else to avoid a night surface engagement that would bring the big guns of the enemy battleships to bear on American vessels with inferior armament and crews ill prepared for night combat.

Once Fletcher's now carrierless task force joined his, Spruance led the American fleet eastward until just after midnight, thereby dashing Yamamoto's last faint hope of a night battle. After Fletcher had detached to search for downed flight crews, Spruance reversed course so that by daylight he would be poised to defend Midway against invasion or to strike at a retreating Japanese force. Fletcher and his overcrowded ships continued southeast toward a fueling rendezvous and to meet the vessel sent out from Pearl to transport the *Yorktown* crew ashore.

As a result, through much of the long night after the battle, the *Yorktown* and the *Hughes* lay closer to the enemy than did any other surface ships in the American fleet.

WHEN THE JAPANESE SUBMARINE *I-168* SURFACED JUST OFF MIDWAY AT 0130 ON JUNE 5, Lt. Comdr. Yahachi Tanabe and his crew as yet knew nothing of the disastrous turn in Japanese fortunes. Tanabe's most recent order from Admiral Yamamoto had instructed him to "shell and destroy the enemy airbase," an impossible task for a solo sub. In the event, Tanabe managed only six rounds before searchlights ashore picked him out, forcing an immediate dive. When he resurfaced soon after dawn, an American ship spotted him and initiated pursuit. The Japanese sub commander, who knew his business, easily shook off his enemy pursuers.

The next time the *I-168* surfaced, Tanabe learned of the sinking of Nagumo's four carriers. He and his crew had observed and cheered the dawn attack on Midway. The news of the fleet's defeat came as a crushing blow.

Tanabe's gloom soon evaporated, however. Cruiser-launched Japanese scout planes had found a *Yorktown*-class carrier drifting without power about 150 miles northeast of Midway. Now the submarine captain received an order that lifted his

The *I-168* (here numbered *I-68*) was part of the striking force's submarine screen, charged with attacking any large units of the American fleet that came its way. As of June 5, however, it had not yet engaged the enemy.

spirits. "Submarine *I-168* will locate and destroy the American carrier." The last offensive gesture by the Japanese at Midway would fall to him and him alone—an unpredictable turn for a submarine commander whose original mission had been to scout the atoll and report on the inevitable success of Japanese air attacks. The *I-168*'s skipper did not pause to ponder his weighty new responsibility. He immediately set course for the enemy carrier's reported position.

One wonders whether Admiral Yamamoto, astride his massive battleship, truly expected a lone submarine to salvage some compensatory glory from the terrible defeat of June 4. Regardless, he had already realized that he had lost his chance to lure the Americans into a second battle. Soon after midnight the Japanese commander in chief canceled plans for a final thrust against Midway, an ill-considered bombardment by four heavy cruisers that would have left them exposed to daylight attacks from both land- and carrier-based bombers. Then, at 0255, he ordered all his forces to retire—all except Commander Tanabe and his valiant crew.

AT DAWN'S FIRST LIGHT ON JUNE 5, ONLY THE DESTROYER *HUGHES* STOOD GUARD OVER THE sharply listing *Yorktown*. Listing, but not about to capsize, concluded *Hughes*'s commanding officer, Lt. Comdr. Donald J. Ramsey, as he contemplated sending a salvage party on board to recover any secret and confidential material left behind in the haste of abandonment. As the sun rose in a cerulean sky, over quiet seas, the previous day's battle seemed impossibly remote.

At 0741, a lookout spotted splashes in the water on the *Yorktown*'s port side—machine-gun fire. Captain Ramsey immediately brought his destroyer alongside to investigate. Aft on the port side of the hangar deck, now almost level with the water, a man was waving weakly. The *Hughes* lowered a motor whaleboat. Slowly the destroyer circled the ship to look for other signs of life while the whaleboat crew boarded the listing carrier to find the stranded seaman.

They brought back Seaman 2nd Class Norman Pichette, who was suffering from severe abdominal wounds and who claimed that he and another man had been left in the battle-dressing station where both had spent the night. This was Seaman 1st Class George Weise, out of action with a badly fractured skull. When Pichette had left him,

The *Hughes* was one of the destroyers that stood guard during attempts to salvage the crippled *Yorktown*.

Weise was unconscious but breathing. A second rescue party boarded the ship and returned with the other wounded man.

Pichette eventually succumbed to his wounds and was buried at sea, but Weise recovered. The *Hughes* would subsequently rescue one more *Yorktown* survivor, Ens. Harry Gibbs, who had spent the better part of a day in a life raft after his Wildcat was shot down during the June 4 battle.

Later that morning, when a search party from the *Hughes* explored the carrier, it returned with three mail sacks packed with code and cipher equipment, more evidence of the undisciplined nature of the *Yorktown*'s abandonment—the bags were found floating in the seawater now washing the decks—along with a cache of classified material from the ship's code room. But the *Hughes*'s salvage party discovered no one else alive. Pichette's death would bring the *Yorktown*'s total losses to 54, not including the 32 aviators lost in the carrier battle.

Word that the *Yorktown* was still afloat buoyed Captain Buckmaster. On board the *Astoria*, he and Admiral Fletcher quickly agreed that salvage operations should be attempted. Forming an effective salvage party presented a distinct challenge, however, since Buckmaster's crew was scattered among several destroyers. (As a result of the *Yorktown*'s experience, every U.S. carrier would henceforth carry a designated salvage group that would remain on board until the last possible minute during an abandonment and be kept together in case it could return. Had such a crew boarded the *Yorktown* on the morning of June 5, her story might have reached a very different conclusion.)

It took most of the morning to transfer the *Yorktown*'s crew from the destroyers to Fletcher's two cruisers. The salvage party assembled on the *Astoria*, the rest on the *Portland* for subsequent transfer to the submarine tender *Fulton*, which had been dispatched from Pearl for this purpose. Bill Surgi, Gordon Skinner, Pete Newberg, Bill Leonard, and Vane Bennett would not see their ship again. John Greenbacker, who was included in the salvage team, recalls that "everyone wanted to go, and finally guards had to be placed at the highlines to keep additional personnel from coming over to the *Astoria* in the determination to go back to their ship. The dedication to the 'Old Lady' was most impressive."

On Fletcher's order, Captain Buckmaster assumed command of a task unit,

consisting of the destroyers *Hammann*, *Balch*, and *Benham*, charged with trying to save the badly damaged carrier. By mid-afternoon, the salvage party had boarded the *Hammann*. At 1800, the three destroyers headed for the *Yorktown*'s position. Buckmaster hoped to be back on board soon after the sun had risen.

IN THE EARLY MORNING BLACKNESS OF JUNE 6, A LOOKOUT ON THE SUBMARINE *I-168* SPOTTED a "black shape on the horizon, 11 miles distant" with the sub's powerful 12 cm binoculars. "It was the easiest intercept a submarine commander ever made," wrote Yahachi

Tanabe many years later. "My course had not changed from beginning to end." Tanabe ordered an immediate dive to a depth of 90 feet, then proceeded toward the target. As the range closed, he reduced his speed to three knots, which gave him maximum maneuverability at the cost of minimum propeller noise. (Unfortunately for the Americans, the rising sea made listening conditions unfavorable.) Every so often, he rose to periscope depth just long enough to adjust his course. As dawn approached he could make out several destroyers forming a protective perimeter around the American ship. Another, the minesweeper-turned-tug *Vireo*, had the carrier under tow.

If he could get inside the destroyer ring, he would have a clear broadside shot at ideal range.

(Opposite) Coal bags carry the *Yorktown*'s crewmen two by two from the heavy cruiser *Portland* to the submarine tender *Fulton*. Aboard the *Portland* (top) crewmen wait their turn to make the trip. (Above) On board the *Fulton*, a seaman takes the roll call of survivors.

ABOUT TWO HOURS AFTER SUNRISE, CAPTAIN BUCKMASTER LED HIS handpicked salvage party on board the *Yorktown*. Meanwhile, the *Balch* and the *Benham* joined the *Hughes*, which had already been joined by the destroyers *Gwin* and *Monaghan* in a defensive screen with a radius of 2,000 yards around the carrier. After briefly joining this screen, the *Hammann* was directed to stand just off the *Yorktown*'s starboard bow to provide hoses and water to put out a fire that had been burning in the rag stowage locker located beneath the forward elevator since the day of the battle. But the *Hammann*'s skipper, Comdr. Arnold True, soon concluded that it was "impossible to lie clear of the *Yorktown* and maintain position accurately enough to permit effective assistance." Accordingly he brought his destroyer neatly along the carrier's high (starboard) side, cushioning his hull with fenders and splinter mattresses. Now he could provide the salvage crews with pumping power for both fire fighting and counterflooding, or filling empty tanks on the high side of the ship to correct its list.

Chief Machinist's Mate John D. Miller, who ordinarily ran the ship's machine shop and had been on board the *Yorktown* since her commissioning in 1937, was one of those assigned the task of locating voids for counterflooding on the high side of the ship, removing their covers, and inserting pump hoses so that they could begin to be filled with seawater. He never forgot the eerie atmosphere of the ship's deserted corridors as he groped his way by the light of a battle lantern. The air belowdecks was stale and the absence of the accustomed ship sounds just plain spooky. "On board the *Yorktown* you had this constant noise," Miller remembers, "that I'd been used to for years—the blowers bringing in fresh air, the steam lines making their whistling/sizzling noises, the fire and flushing lines being repeatedly flushed, the loudspeakers crackling with commands." Now "the silence was deafening." The sound of his boots on the metal decks echoed eerily, as if he were walking inside a huge empty tank car.

Throughout the ship, the salvage parties set to work. Topside crews worked to jettison any object that weighed down the low port side—airplanes, guns, anchors. Belowdecks, in addition to the men fighting fires and counterflooding the ship, a team combed the most sensitive areas for any remaining secret material. Lieutenant Greenbacker's "chief responsibility was to go about the ship and secure all confidential publications. The larger part of these were aviators' contact codes, some 70 of which were scattered about the ready rooms," he recalls. "I gradually gathered them up and

One of the very few photographs taken on board during the attempt to salvage the *Yorktown* on the morning of June 6, this image shows crewmen on the hangar deck preparing to jettison a plane overboard, probably the spare Devastator from the ship's torpedo squadron.

locked them in the vault, incidentally picking up a few choice items such as winter flight boots and cold-weather flight jackets." What with the heat and stuffiness, Greenbacker found working his way through the awkwardly canted corridors exhausting.

"In the mid-afternoon, I was directed by Lieutenant-Commander Ray [the ship's communications officer] to help him assemble Admiral Fletcher's message files, which we removed from the safe in the flag plot. With these packed into a mailbag, we proceeded to the quarterdeck area, where I was to transfer to the *Hammann* and go by the *Hammann*'s boat to deliver the bag to one of the destroyers, which was scheduled to depart that afternoon for Pearl Harbor. On the quarterdeck, someone had placed several cases of Coca-Cola and it was for one of these that I stopped before proceeding to the *Hammann*."

By this time the salvagers had improved the *Yorktown*'s list from 24° to 22°. This, combined with the water pumped overboard or from flooded areas on the port side to voids on the ship's higher starboard side, had reduced by three feet the water level on the third deck. If only a larger fleet tug had arrived, the *Yorktown* might already have been making headway toward Pearl Harbor. The straining *Vireo* could barely budge what was, in effect, a badly listing barge displacing 20,000 tons. The ex-minesweeper was able to do little more than hold the huge carrier's bow into the freshening wind and rising seas.

COMMANDER TANABE COULD ONLY WONDER AT HIS APPARENT GOOD FORTUNE, A SITUATION he attributed more to American incompetence than to the Shinto shrine charms his chief electrical officer—"a deeply religious man"—had presented to each member of the crew during a recent shore leave. So far the Americans had failed to detect his presence. Now, for some inexplicable reason, they seemed to have turned off their sound-listening equipment.

"'It appears the Americans have interrupted their war for lunch,'" Tanabe later wrote he had commented. "'Now is our chance to strike them good and hard, while they are eating!' There were small jokes made about what we could give her for dessert."

The *I-168* had successfully sneaked beneath the American destroyer screen, but when Tanabe ascended to periscope depth, he discovered that he was too close to the carrier, only 600 yards or so, for his torpedoes to reach the correct depth before impact. With his heart in his throat, he dived deeper again and made an achingly slow turn that would bring him into a better position—if the destroyers did not finally sniff him out. Meanwhile he concocted a plan to maximize the destructive force of his weapons. Because the enemy target was, for all practical purposes, stationary, Tanabe could risk firing his four torpedoes in two tight bursts. Torpedoes one and two would follow one after another along the same course; torpedoes three and four would likewise be paired. "That way, I could achieve two large hits instead of four small ones," he reasoned.

"When I was back on my approach course, I took another look and wagged my head at how the destroyers still seemed unaware of us. Either they were poor sailors, had poor equipment, or *I-168* was a charmed vessel. At a range of 1,200 yards, my periscope up, I sent my four torpedoes away as planned. I did not lower the periscope then, either. The wakes of my torpedoes could be seen, so their source could be quickly established. And if *I-168* was going to die, I at least wanted the satisfaction of seeing whether our fish hit home. Less than a minute later, we hear the explosions.

"'*Banzai!*' someone shouted.

"'Go ahead full speed!' I ordered, then, 'Take her down 200 feet!'"

LIEUTENANT GREENBACKER WAS TAKING ONE LAST SIP OF HIS COKE BEFORE CROSSING THE gangway to the *Hammann* when his "pleasant pause was interrupted by the sudden firing of our 20 mm alarm gun, cries of 'Torpedoes!' and the buzzing of *Hammann*'s general alarm. My reaction was unthinking. I immediately fled with my mail sack to the port side of the quarterdeck. By the time I reached it, I had time to reflect that perhaps torpedoes might be coming from that side also and that I was awfully close to the water. As a result of this thought, I secured the bag to the ship's structure and then by means of lines that lay across the hangar deck worked my way back uphill to midships, where it seemed I had forever to wait for the torpedoes to hit. But they finally came with the usual muffled explosion and the slow, tremendous heave of the deck."

The force of the three torpedo detonations threw many men off their feet. From his

position amidships, Greenbacker heard calls for help from Lt. Albert H. Wilson, who was trapped under a hatch to the hangar deck from which he'd been emerging just as the torpedoes struck. The junior officer freed Wilson, who didn't seem to be injured, then continued aft to the quarterdeck just in time to see "the *Hammann* settling in the water on an even keel. She gave me the impression of a ship that might have been dropped from a great height, upright but broken. She sank smoothly, submerging rather evenly and plunging forward with her fantail disappearing last. When the entire ship was well underwater, all of her depth charges exploded in a tremendous explosion." (In fact, many of her depth charges were disarmed before she sank.) As he would later joke, that Coca-Cola—the "pause that refreshes"—saved his life.

When *I-168*'s commander raised his periscope, he saw the *Yorktown* virtually dead in the water ahead of him, with the *Hammann* alongside. Quickly, he fired four torpedoes.

(Next page) The Japanese torpedoes hit the *Yorktown* and the *Hammann*.

When the torpedoes struck, Chief Machinist's Mate John Miller was removing the cover of a void tank whose opening was located in one of the offices on the second deck of the starboard side of the ship, outboard of the stack. The *Yorktown*'s navigator, Comdr. Irving D. Wiltsie, was lending him a hand. The intense vibration from the explosion did something to Miller's knees, but the pain was manageable. "It was like when you sprain an ankle," he recalls. "You know something is wrong but you just keep going. I didn't know anything was wrong until about two weeks later when my knees started swelling up." The doctor would tell him that both his kneecaps were laced with hairline fractures.

Comdr. Wiltsie seemed to be unhurt and both men were able to make their way topside where they joined the exodus to the *Vireo*, which had quickly cut its tow line and skillfully come alongside to remove the salvage crew. Ironically, the first effect of the torpedo hits was to correct the *Yorktown*'s list another 5°. More ominously, however, the ship had also settled more deeply into the water.

The first of the *I-168*'s torpedoes ran shallow and slammed into the *Hammann*, which sank in five minutes. The next two penetrated the *Yorktown*'s hull. The fourth narrowly missed. A remarkable proportion of the *Hammann*'s crew escaped their sinking vessel, only to face the shock of the exploding depth charges. C. M. Lee, Jr., the medical officer on the *Balch* who came aboard the *Benham* to tend to the injured, vividly described the result: "With the exception of a few men who were in, or succeeded in getting into, a boat that was just leaving the *Hammann* at the time the torpedoes struck, every man rescued was injured to some degree by the underwater explosions. The men were soaked with fuel oil, and all were prostrated by submersion, chill, and the shock of the explosions. A total of 173 men and 5 officers were taken on board. Of these, 18 were already dead or died shortly thereafter, and 5 more succumbed during the ensuing 14 to 16 hours. Some 10 to 15 men were suffering from fractures in various locations, probably sustained at the time of the torpedo explosions, and one had extensive burns to his face, arms, and throat, and this entire burned area was thickly covered with salt.

"Of the remaining men, the type of injury was horrible in its uniformity . . . . Treatment was, of course, limited to supportive measures. Initially the problem was one of seeing that each man was given morphine and covered with blankets. The decks, passages,

wardroom, and officers' rooms were so littered with prostrate men that it was difficult to move around without stepping on them."

While the survivors from the *Hammann* were being pulled from the water, Captain Buckmaster ordered the *Yorktown* abandoned for the second time. The *Vireo* came alongside and the transfer began. When it appeared everyone was on board, Captain Buckmaster "climbed down the line to the deck of the tug," remembered Lieutenant Greenbacker. "Almost immediately thereafter, there appeared on the quarterdeck the chief engineer, Commander Delaney, and two of his men who had been below.

(Left and opposite) The last moments of the *Hammann* were captured by Photographer's Mate 2nd Class William G. Roy, who was part of the salvage party aboard the *Yorktown*. Many of the *Hammann*'s crew who managed to escape the ship's sinking were killed or wounded in the water when her depth charges went off.

Thereupon Buckmaster, who was tremendously upset by thus having been deprived of being the last to leave the ship, attempted to swing back on a line and touch the *Yorktown* .... In the end, the tug cast off before the captain was able to make it."

But the *Yorktown*'s skipper had not yet given up all hope of salvaging his vessel. He planned to return at first light on the morrow.

COMMANDER TANABE LED THREE AMERICAN DESTROYERS A MERRY CHASE FOR THE TWO HOURS following his attack on the *Yorktown* and the *Hammann*. For a while he hid beneath the carrier. When he tried to sneak away, the enemy was on him immediately, dropping depth charges in ones and twos. Quickly he learned to turn and race toward each destroyer as it moved to attack. Time and again his sub would pass beneath and beyond the enemy vessel, so that the depth charges detonated safely astern. Tanabe counted 60 explosions before one finally blew up too close to his bow. The hull sprang many small leaks, the ship's lights went out, and most seriously of all, two of the torpedo tubes were opened to the sea. His crew worked feverishly to seal off the affected compartments. By the time this work was completed, the *I-168* was badly down at the bow.

Tanabe ordered all crew aft, but this produced only a negligible correction in trim. Then he resorted to a simple but effective tactic that had been tried by other submarine commanders during the war. Each crewman walked forward, picked up a bag of rice from the food storage locker and carried it aft. By the time electrical power had been restored, the sub was back at equilibrium. Now a far more serious problem faced its captain.

After almost 12 hours submerged, the *I-168* had all but exhausted its batteries, which could be recharged only by running along the surface. The depth-charge attacks had tailed off, but the occasional nearby detonation confirmed the Americans had not given up the chase. They had probably calculated he would soon need to surface and were waiting to pounce. Tanabe bided his time, watching the battery gauges drop toward

zero while oxygen sank near the danger point. The American firing stopped. More minutes passed. Perhaps the enemy had departed. Tanabe decided to risk resurfacing.

The sun sat low in the western sky, its long light illuminating three destroyers about 11,000 yards to the east. They were heading east where the *Yorktown* had been. The American carrier had either sunk or was beyond the eastern horizon. Maybe he could slip away.

Tanabe stood on the platform atop the conning tower flanked by lookouts armed with pistols and rifles from the armory, directing the helmsman by voice tube. He ran west as fast as he could, at 14 knots. He had been spotted. Two of the three American destroyers turned to follow.

The *I-168* made smoke and continued running along the surface at top speed. Slowly the battery needles inched upward. For some reason, destroyers capable of more than twice his speed didn't seem to be gaining. Ten minutes. Twenty minutes. In fact, the enemy *was* gaining, and still he needed more time before he could safely submerge. Thirty minutes. The two destroyers had closed to about 6,500 yards. They began firing. Soon two salvos straddled the sub. The enemy gunners had found the range.

"I can remember the moment of the straddle most vividly," Tanabe later wrote. "My lookouts began darting quick looks at me, their faces strained and pale. They

Midway Finale

On the morning of June 6, while the submarine *I-168* stalked the *Yorktown*, carrier-based dive-bombers delivered the final American blows of the battle. Planes from the *Hornet* and the *Enterprise* jumped the Japanese heavy cruiser *Mikuma*, which was retreating with three other cruisers and two destroyers from their canceled mission to bombard Midway. The *Mikuma*'s travails had begun in the early morning of June 5. While taking evasive action after spotting a surfaced American submarine, her sister ship the *Mogami* sliced into the *Mikuma*'s side, crumpling her own bow and tearing a big hole in the *Mikuma*'s port side that ruptured her fuel oil tanks. Leaving both destroyers to escort the two damaged cruisers, the rest of the task group retired. By daylight on June 5, the *Mikuma*'s trail of leaking fuel oil led Midway-based bombers to the target, although they did little damage. On June 6, the dive-bomber crews were much luckier, leaving the ship a smoldering wreck. That evening, she turned over and sank, taking nearly a thousand men with her.

Dive-bombers from the *Hornet* (top) took part in the June 6 attacks on the limping Japanese cruiser *Mikuma*, which was soon set afire (center) and, after listing badly (above), subsequently rolled over and sank.

were anxious to be back in the hull and diving. I could also detect a high note in the voices below as reports on the progress of the battery charge were called up to me. The men above wanted to dive, though they dared not say so, and the men below wanted to remain surfaced as long as possible while dials and gauges made higher readings.

"Finally, the enemy silhouettes growing ever larger, I called down, 'Do you have enough air and power for short-time operations?'

"A reluctant 'Yes, sir' came up.

"'Stand by to dive!' I shouted, and cleared the bridge."

Tanabe's final evasive tactic worked like a Shinto charm. He turned and dived into his own smoke. The pursuing destroyers ran over and past him. By the time they relocated the sub, sunset had almost come. Over the listening phones, he could hear the enemy propeller noise fading away to the east. Perhaps the American destroyers feared a night engagement.

Safely past sunset, the *I-168* surfaced on an empty sea. Now, if only Commander Tanabe had enough fuel to get him home.

THROUGH THE NIGHT OF JUNE 6–7, FIVE DESTROYERS AND ONE TUG MAINTAINED A SILENT vigil for the *Yorktown*, circling at a respectful distance of 4,000 yards. By the hour before dawn, the carrier's list to port was so pronounced that swells washed onto the flight deck like waves lapping on a beach. As daylight rose, the list increased.

Every man who could walk mustered topside for the *Yorktown*'s final farewell. Every flag dipped its colors to half-mast. At 0458, the *Yorktown* "turned over on her port side and sank in about 3,000 fathoms of water with all battle flags flying," according to Captain Buckmaster's official report.

"We watched the Old Lady roll over and sink," Greenbacker later wrote. "Some internal deck or bulkhead, weakened by the heavy series of blows, had finally given way. For us of the salvage party, the Battle of Midway was over."

Just as Haruo Yoshino and Yuji Akamatsu had wept at the sinking of the *Kaga*, so John Miller and John Greenbacker and many of their shipmates wept as the *Yorktown* went down. Greenbacker, who with the rest of the salvage party had spent the night on the *Vireo*, remembers glancing up to the bridge of the minesweeper-turned-tug to see Captain Buckmaster standing stock-still against the morning sky. Nobody spoke. There was nothing to say.

"We saluted her," recalled Lt. Comdr. Clarence "Jug" Ray, "and I'm sure the tears that came from Captain Buckmaster's eyes were no more salty than my own."

John Miller still gets choked up when he recalls the *Yorktown*'s final moments. "I can tell you—and I'm not going to lie—that I had tears in my eyes. Because that ship had been my home.... I've been on a lot of ships, a lot of ships since then, and I never felt, ever, on any of the others, the camaraderie that existed on the *Yorktown*."

Then, like hushed mourners at the funeral of someone who has died far too young, the ships dispersed, the *Vireo* to Midway, the rest, including the *Benham* with the survivors from the *Hammann* on board, to Pearl Harbor.

As this chapter of the Battle of Midway drew to its wistful close, the defeated armada of the Japanese Imperial Fleet continued its long trip home, having squandered its one great chance to deal the American Navy a crippling early blow. Yuji Akamatsu remembers that shameful journey: "The destroyer was so crowded that we had to sleep on the decks. By the end, the food was running low. I don't remember talking or sleeping at all."

The aftershocks of battle would reverberate through the lives of all who participated and survived. Because of the loss of the *Yorktown*, Frank Jack Fletcher's star began to fall. He would come in for even greater, and equally unjustified, criticism during the landings at Guadalcanal in August and during the Battle of the Eastern Solomons later the same month. In fall 1942 he would be reassigned to a shore command and would close out the war in a lesser Pacific combat role, his star eclipsed by his number two at Midway. He would never command a carrier task force again.

Admiral Spruance never looked back. Good luck and good timing vaulted him to the leadership of America's fast-expanding Fifth Fleet, which soon hopelessly outnumbered the Japanese as it pushed the island-hopping American advance toward Tokyo.

Admiral Nagumo continued to exercise command until June 1944, when he perished on the island of Saipan during the American invasion, probably a suicide. Admiral Yamaguchi's suicide as the *Hiryu* went down deprived him of any chance of

**The foundering *Yorktown* turned over just before she sank,
revealing some of the torpedo damage that had sealed her fate.**

succeeding Isoroku Yamamoto, whose career came crashing to an end in April 1943, less than a year after Midway, when American fighters jumped his airplane over Buin, thanks to another break in Japanese intelligence.

And what of the four men who would return to Midway 56 years after the fact to face their memories and make peace with them? Harry Ferrier recovered completely from his head wound and joined Torpedo Squadron Three, which was reassigned to the *Enterprise*. Two months after the Midway battle, he helped cover the American landings at Guadalcanal. But he never again sat in the tunnel gunner's seat. "I figured that if I was going to get shot at again, I wanted to see who was shooting at me," he says. Ferrier stayed with the Navy after World War II, seeing active duty in both the Korean and Vietnam Wars.

Bill Surgi's war briefly had him serving on the brand-new *Essex*-class carrier, the *Yorktown*, then on its sister, the new *Lexington*, namesakes of the co-combatants at the Battle of the Coral Sea. He was on the *Lexington* when she was torpedoed during a December 1943 raid on the Marshall Islands and again suffered minor injuries. He left the Navy in 1950 to join his father's business but re-enlisted in 1953 and added another 11 years of active service.

After the war Yuji Akamatsu and Haruo Yoshino took up their civilian lives in their shattered country. Both married, raised families, and had successful careers. Yoshino became a middle-level executive in an insurance firm. Akamatsu took over his family's fish-processing business.

Their lives followed different paths, but all shared one certainty. The ships and planes lost at the battle of Midway would never be seen again.

Chapter Seven
Three Miles Down

Friday, May 15, 1998

IN MY DREAM, I'M STANDING AT THE PODIUM IN EXPLORERS HALL AT NATIONAL Geographic headquarters in Washington, D.C., squinting into the television lights, blinking back at the camera flashes. My wife, Barbara, sits smiling proudly in the front row, cradling our infant daughter, Emily Rose, who isn't fussing a bit. Beside her sits my grown-up son, Douglas, with my five-year-old son, Ben, in his lap. The room is packed with media. Just the way it was after the *Titanic*, after the *Bismarck*. I'm about to announce my latest discovery to the world. I clear my throat and begin.

"On a June day in 1942, the United States of America fought and won one of the greatest battles in the history of naval warfare, a battle that forever transformed the nature of conflict at sea. In May 1998, almost 56 years later, we returned to this epic field of battle to search for five great ships—four Japanese aircraft carriers and one American aircraft carrier—that sank at Midway.

(Opposite) As the ATV begins a descent to the ocean floor, its lights eerily illuminate the underwater world.

"Sadly, the Japanese carriers eluded us, just as they dodged wave after wave of American attack planes during the first hours of June 4, 1942. Above all I wanted to find the *Kaga*, the ship of the two Japanese veterans who accompanied our expedition. I wanted to give them a chance to close the circle of their lives. I'm deeply disappointed that I failed to do so. And I want to apologize to Haruo Yoshino and Yuji Akamatsu, two gallant warriors, for having let them down.

"There were many times during this expedition that I feared we would come home empty-handed, that our four weeks spent sailing the isolated waters off Midway would add up to nothing. Today, however, I'm pleased to show you the first images of U.S.S. *Yorktown* seen in 56 years. She looks almost as proud as she did when she put up her incredible fight to stay afloat following the battle.

"Ladies and gentleman, I give you the *Yorktown.*"

As the lights dim, the huge white screen looms behind me. I click the remote control for the slide projector. The screen is illuminated with a rectangle of empty white light. Someone must have loaded the carousel improperly. I click again. Nothing. I click again and again, faster and faster. Nothing. Nothing. Nothing. The blank screen seems to grow bigger and bigger. I'm clicking faster than the projector can possibly go. The screen seems to be advancing toward me ....

I WOKE UP BATHED IN SWEAT, WITH THE SHEET OVER MY HEAD.

The motion of the ship was different: The sea was getting rougher. If this meant our luck was changing, it didn't seem to be changing for the better.

I got dressed and went topside. Sure enough, the wind had increased and the seas were between five and six feet. These swells are nothing like those we regularly experience in the North Atlantic, even in summer, but in our flat-bottomed boat they guarantee a rough ride—and a tougher launching for the ATV—if the camera vehicle doesn't break down on us again. (I must have known in my bones that our technical problems weren't over.)

The stopover at Midway lasted longer than I wanted or planned. I was itching to get back to the *Yorktown* site, to prove to myself—and to the world—that our primary sonar target was really the ship. It took almost two full days to make the repairs the ATV needed. And we're still waiting for the titanium spheres we ordered to replace the pressure spheres that wrecked the ATV back in Week One. While we waited, I took everyone out for a wonderful French meal at the one restaurant on the island. Efforts are being made to turn Midway into an ecotourism destination, but we pretty much had the restaurant to ourselves. After a few glasses of wine and some fabulous food, everyone was in a great mood, feeling confident that it was only a matter of sending the vehicle down to the *Yorktown* target for a look at the ship. This brought my doubts back—in spades.

Back at sea the deteriorating weather soon turned the mood on the ship cranky—with the shining exception of Bill Surgi, who always seems to be in good spirits. Undoubtedly he's got another project on the go. I'm sure he's planning something for when we find the ship. *If* we find the ship.

What really upset a lot of people today was the discovery that one of the Navy navigators—due perhaps to some notion of military security—had changed our

As we headed back out to the *Yorktown* site, I wondered whether our primary target would be the lost aircraft carrier or just another example of deep-ocean geology. In a matter of hours, pictures from the ATV would give us the answer.

sea-going e-mail address without bothering to tell anyone. E-mail is our lifeline out here. Now I'm wondering how much traffic got lost in the ether. I broke one of my cardinal rules of command and lost my temper with the officer in charge. I won't do it again. (Our e-mail, however, is back on line.)

We arrived back at the *Yorktown* site early this afternoon and within minutes had begun the pre-dive routine, checking each system before the lowering. Almost immediately the Navy reported more problems, which meant we had to scratch today's dive while they tried to figure things out.

Saturday, May 16

THIS MORNING MY GLOOM LIFTED WITH THE WEATHER. PETER SCHNALL FILMED ME ON THE bow talking about our prospects of finding the ship. I was really feeling confident.

"It feels good," I told him. "For a couple of weeks the *Yorktown* has been fighting us, but today it feels right. Feels calm. I think the *Yorktown* is ready to let us see her. We'll find out pretty soon."

Our historian, Chuck Haberlein, has even brought along a good-luck charm to help combat our apparent technical curse: it's a plush toy Laysan albatross he bought on Midway. Like me, Chuck noticed how the black-footed albatrosses were landing beside the ATV before every launch. Like me, he began to wonder if perhaps they were jinxing our mission. I was happy to have every bit of help I could get, joke or not.

Now, at the end of another long and frustrating day, I have to eat my morning's optimism. Finally, at 1615, the ATV was on its way down. A few minutes later a routine check of the National Geographic Society's remotely triggered camera—the gizmo that's supposed to take all the still pictures of the wreck—showed it to be inoperative. Since the vehicle was still near the surface, I decided to recover it, remove the camera, and get it fixed. Turned out the trigger was flooded. What next?

By early evening the ATV was again on the way down. For how long? I decided to catch up on my log and then snatch a few hours' sleep.

Sunday, May 17

THE NIGHTMARE CONTINUES. TODAY THE ATV LOST ITS TELEMETRY ON THE WAY DOWN, SO we hauled it back on deck for the Navy to reterminate the cable. Another wait—24 to 36 hours—precious time slipping away. When will the problems end? In ten days, we must be back on Midway preparing to fly home. What started out looking like a slam dunk is beginning to look like a game that may not even get started.

Bill Surgi wants the *Yorktown* as badly as I do. He wants the *Yorktown* for his buddies, the ones who lived and the ones who died. I want it for him. And for them.

Monday, May 18

I T'S NEARING MIDNIGHT AND STILL THE VEHICLE ISN'T BACK IN THE WATER. WATCHING PAINT dry is nothing compared to waiting for epoxy to cure. Sometime in the next few hours—that's what Chief Swarm and his Navy crew are promising. This is like Chinese water torture. I've got to try to get some rest. Tomorrow. Maybe tomorrow.

All day I kept turning the data over and over in my mind. Always it said the same thing: The target must be the *Yorktown*. But the doubts keep creeping back in. Admiral Morison's position and the one from the Naval War College both have the ship sinking ten miles north of here on top of a seamount. And those two Japanese targets seemed so solid, almost as solid as the target three miles below, the target that's teasing us to death. But neither of those two had been covered as exhaustively by the

sonar before we dived. That's what I keep telling myself.

No, this has got to be it. The data base is too solid. The target is too perfect—the size and height of the *Yorktown* if it is sitting upright in the mud with 45 feet of the hull exposed.

Or it could be a *Yorktown*-size ridge of volcanic rock?

Tuesday, May 19

I AWOKE AT 0600. THE *LANEY* WAS QUIET EXCEPT FOR THE USUAL SHIP noises and the clatter of pots in the galley. I had no idea whether the ATV was on the bottom or still sitting on the fantail.

I sat up and looked out my viewport. Lt. Jay Dryer, (the Navy exec, or executive officer), was standing at the rail near the ATV control van, staring out to the horizon. I jumped immediately to the conclusion that the vehicle was back on deck with yet another one of its endless series of problems. This was no way to win a war.

I didn't bother to dress, just threw on my sweats and headed to the War Room. The dry lab was deserted except for Cathy Offinger, who greeted me cheerfully.

"The vehicle is at 16,000 and going down," she told me. "We're almost there."

Briefly I wondered if this was another one of my dreams— about to go sour. But I could smell coffee coming from the galley. I headed back to my cabin to shower and shave and dress. It was time to face the music, and I wanted to be ready to conduct the band.

I was still getting dressed when Cathy knocked on my door to tell me the ATV's sonar was picking up two strong targets. I grabbed a Coke and headed back to the lab, and what I saw didn't encourage me: The remote sonar display showed two strong targets, all right, but they were soft and round-looking, clearly pieces of sloping bottom surface. Nothing man-made. I nipped across the deck, up the ladder, along the hangar, and into the control van. I didn't even notice if the sun was shining. Inside the van, the dim light seemed tense, not comforting. Jay Minkin had turned on the video, which was showing only a deep blue expanse of nothing. Peter was already filming. If this was it, he wasn't going to miss a moment. I took my usual spot on the upended trash can, behind the ATV pilot and co-pilot. Here we go again, I thought to myself as I turned my eyes to the video screen.

The pilot, holding the joystick, was having trouble controlling

(Above) The ATV slips beneath the waves. (Below) A potential target appears on the sonar screen in the ATV's control van.

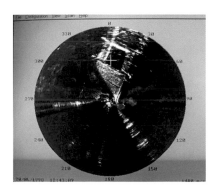

the ATV. Then he pulled in some cable, causing the vehicle to move backward. As it did so, the down-looking camera picked up a small target, perhaps a piece of wreckage. Elsewhere the bottom was covered with manganese nodules, which are fascinating geologically—but there was no time to think about them now. I could smell the ship.

The pilot slowly began to gain control of the ATV, and we began driving east toward the target. In a few moments we would know whether the *MR-1* team had really discovered the *Yorktown* among all the perplexing sonar data.

As we crept along the bottom, the ATV's forward-looking sonar began picking up a series of small targets. The *pings* began to elide into a kind of whooshing whistle. On the sonar, the targets looked to me like big pieces of debris. Then I saw the mud ball.

The first time I'd seen a mud ball like this one was near the *Titanic*, a huge clod of bottom sediment kicked up by the force of the ship's tremendous impact. Ocean geologists refer to this phenomenon by the rather unexciting label of "impact splatter." But there was nothing unexciting about this particular example. Unless a meteorite had landed nearby, we were close to a huge object of human origin. Something the size of an aircraft carrier.

As we moved forward, the area of splatter quickly gave way to a wide swath of the bottom that appeared to have been bulldozed clean of those nodules of manganese. To my eye, I was unquestionably looking at the edge of an impact crater.

"Something hit hard here," I commented. I caught Peter's eye and winked at him. He got the message. As far as I was concerned, we had found the *Yorktown*. "Got it," I said quietly, almost to myself.

Now the sonar was going crazy, wailing like an electronic banshee. A long, sharp image appeared on the ATV's sonar.

"Something. Man-made," I commented with remarkable understatement, my heart racing.

"Holy cow!" Chief Swarm was definitely getting into the spirit.

"Look up. There it is. Stop. Stop. Stop." I was probably speaking a little louder than I needed to, to make myself heard. The van was deathly quiet. Was anyone breathing?

We drew closer still, the ATV's cameras picking up bits of wreckage.

"Thar she blows!" I announced. We were looking at the outline of what surely had to be an aircraft carrier flight deck. "Bingo! Bingo! Bingo!"

If this wasn't the *Yorktown*, then the Battle of Midway never happened.

We slowly rose up the end of the hangar deck, passing over a tangle of catwalk and decking.

We hovered above the sloping flight deck—the ship was still listing. A hole in the middle of the deck had to be either the aft or the forward elevator opening. At this point, Bill Surgi broke in over the intercom from the wet lab where he and a big crowd were watching.

(Above) The guns in two of the *Yorktown*'s quadruple 1.1-inch gun mounts just forward and below the bridge still point skyward as if awaiting enemy attack. (Below left) The main support for the after end of the flight deck rises from the stern. (Below right) Above this, the stern of the flight deck is badly battered.

"While you're there, see if you can find the mural," he told me. He was referring to a mural painted on the wall of No. 2 elevator, a depiction of all the voyages of the *Yorktown* in both hemispheres. Although I wasn't sure where we were, Surgi obviously was. I told him to come down to the van and help us out.

As we continued along the flight deck, the ship's island, its bridge and stack, hove into view. At last we had our bearings for sure (and Bill was right). We had come in over the stern and traveled along the port side of the flight deck. The catwalk looked as if it could still bear human weight. The flight deck showed really remarkably little

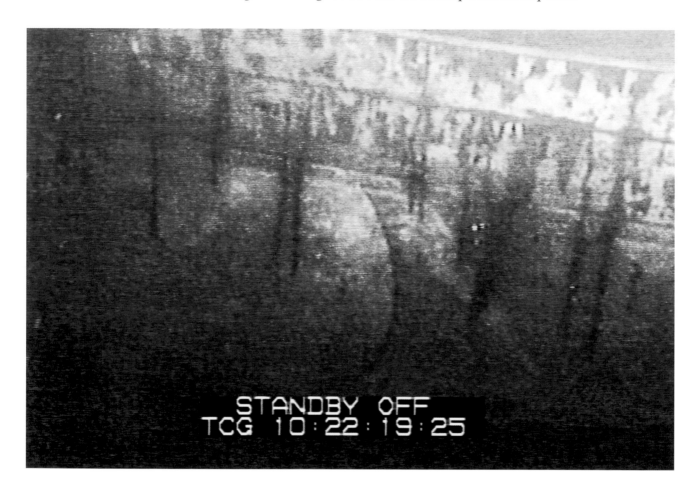

STANDBY OFF
TCG 10:22:19:25

deterioration after 56 years. The whole ship seemed to be in amazingly good shape. It had nothing like the marine growth we had found on the *Titanic*—and less even than was on the *Bismarck*.

A mount of 1.1-inch antiaircraft guns pointed skyward, as if trained on diving Vals.

"Looks like Iron Bottom Sound," I commented, instantly transported to our exploration six years before of the waters off Guadalcanal.

The base of the crane at the aft end of the island was clearly visible. By now Bill, who had been watching on the wet lab video, had joined us in the van. He began to recognize features.

"I'm lookin' at the radio room right now," he said as we began our ascent up the island. We rose up the superstructure. "That's the bridge."

"Too much . . . too much." The emotion of the moment was clearly getting to Bill. "All the people who did their jobs . . . I can see them doing them right now."

All too soon—and all too predictably—it was over. A leaking hydraulics line forced us to terminate the dive when we had barely begun to explore the ship. But there was no question we had found the *Yorktown*. We had finally made it home.

Wednesday, May 20

(Opposite) The ATV's video camera caught a fleeting glimpse of part of what survives of the mural painted on the wall of No. 2 elevator. Details of the globe and searchlight (shown in the 1942 photo above) are still faintly visible.

TODAY WE TOURED U.S.S. *YORKTOWN* FROM STEM TO STERN, FROM mudline to island top. (Not surprisingly, the ship's tripod mast is gone.) After all the frustration, all the false starts, I'm glad to report that today was perfect.

Overall the ship is in stunning shape, given the punishment she took and the depth of her final plunge. She sits upright, with a 25° list to starboard—much the way she looked at sunset on June 6 after the torpedoes from the Japanese submarine sealed her fate, except that back then she was listing to port. We looked into a big torpedo hole amidships on the port side, probably the combined result of the two airplane-launched torpedoes from the *Hiryu*'s second attack, which struck the ship quite close together. The area of submarine *I-168*'s torpedo damage is below the mudline at the starboard side, which reaches almost as high as the flight deck—possibly evidence the ship was moving sideways when it was hit. We found the hole made by the bomb that wiped out the 1.1-inch gun mount on which Gordon Skinner trained his fire hose. As for Bill Surgi's battle station, that part of the starboard catwalk just aft of the midships elevator has disappeared. But we did catch a glimpse of the mural inside the middle elevator, which looks to be amazingly well preserved.

There's a thin layer of silt on the flight deck, but its wooden surface appears to be intact. This makes an interesting contrast between the deep-ocean biology in the tropical mid-Pacific and the very active organic life at the *Titanic* site. (Only teak, a highly resistant wood, remains on the *Titanic*.) The colder water in the north Atlantic can support more marine life than the water in warmer latitudes. The colder the water, the more nutrients it can absorb. Being farther from a continent, the *Yorktown* is covered with less sediment than the *Titanic*.

I've argued for quite a while that telepresence is better than actually diving on a wreck in a cold, cramped research submersible, but I'm still amazed at how easily the distance between the surface and the wreck disappears. In the darkened van, staring at that video screen, I almost felt I could reach out and touch the ship. But there's always a moment when more than physical distance evaporates, when the divide between past and present melts away.

For starters, a deep-ocean shipwreck has the uncanny knack of seeming very fresh—as if it has just happened. In the case of the *Yorktown*, with so little decay and so little marine encrustation, the sensation was unusually powerful. The paint that still clings to the metal hull in most places showed scorch marks from the battle. The gun barrels still shone; the flight deck still looked as though it could launch a Wildcat or a Dauntless. It was as if we had stumbled on the ship a few minutes after it made its death plunge. The sediment stirred up by its powerful impact had only just settled. There it sat, suspended in time. Timeless.

I could see the years melting away for Bill Surgi when we went looking for his battle station. As we searched that section of the hull, Bill was back in the middle of the battle, seeing the Japanese bombers screaming in, hearing the insane noise of all the antiaircraft guns, watching the Japanese radio gunner who seemed to be waving at him, feeling the upward lurch that broke his arm and impaled his friend David Patterson. (Patterson survived and, after the war, became a longtime member of the *Yorktown* Association until his death a few years ago.)

For me it happened as we zoomed in on one of the gun mounts, the seats for the spotter and the trainer still intact. The men sitting in those seats and firing away for dear life were only boys—17, 18, 19. Even though the *Yorktown* herself lost relatively few, the Battle of Midway took a terrible toll of young men—especially aviators. Their parents mourned as I did when I lost a son of 20. No matter how noble the cause, it can never make any sense.

BEFORE HEADING BACK INTO MIDWAY TO PICK UP THE NEW LIGHTS FOR the ATV, we began our search for the *Hammann*, the destroyer that sank within five minutes of submarine *I-168*'s devastating attack on June 6, 1942. We know that several of the *Yorktown*'s final escorting destroyers reported a current of about 0.5 knots, course 220, during the 17 hours between her final torpedoing and her sinking, which is pretty much the current we've been measuring on our expedition. That means the shattered remnants of the

(Above) Gun tubs loom below as we peer down over the bridge area. (Below) This unexploded depth charge, presumably from the *Hammann,* lay not far from the *Yorktown* wreck.

Hammann should lie somewhat to the northeast of the wreck of the carrier.

Rather than heading directly for the destroyer's estimated sinking site, however, I wanted to search the entire path the *Yorktown* drifted after she was torpedoed. If there was time, we would search farther, hoping to find some of the planes jettisoned during salvage operations on June 6. But we definitely wanted to find the *Hammann*.

We had time to run two search lines before heading into port. Both lines were at right angles to the probable line of drift. Now that our sonar is gone, I've reverted to the search strategy that found both the *Titanic* and the *Bismarck*, a visual search with a deep-towed camera vehicle running lines perpendicular to the expected debris trail. With luck, the debris trail will lead us to the *Hammann*. The lightest debris, which takes the longest to reach the bottom, will be closest to where the *Yorktown* lies. The heaviest—the *Hammann* itself—will be farthest away.

Sure enough, at the end of two search lines, the ATV had found three unexploded depth charges. In all likelihood these fell from the sinking *Hammann*. Since we still have at least four days on site, we should have lots of time to follow this trail to its conclusion.

It's time to hit the rack. I'm exhausted but now it doesn't matter. We've found our wreck and she's a beauty. We've made it through the eye of the needle once again. The gods are smiling.

Monday, May 25 (Memorial Day)

I GUESS CHUCK HABERLEIN'S GOOD-LUCK ALBATROSS HAS A LIMITED-time warranty. In the past four days at the *Yorktown* site, we have once again been plagued by breakdowns and delays. Finally, on May 23, we managed our third and last lowering on the ship. A memorial plaque we had planned to set gently on the flight deck broke loose during the descent and landed who knows where. At least the new lights worked well enough to allow us to take several hundred more color stills and additional high-quality video. The great irony is that the water around the *Yorktown* is so clear that we really didn't need the lights at all. Which means that all the nightmares that began almost four weeks ago when the pressure spheres housing the original batteries imploded could have been avoided. The words "if only" don't capture it, but at times like this that's all you can say.

Yesterday the weather steadily deteriorated. So instead of continuing our search for the *Hammann*, we recovered the vehicle with the hope that today, our last day on site, we would have one more shot. Not a chance. By this morning the storm had worsened. Reluctantly we decided to pull up stakes—in this case, transponders—and head for home.

Before we left we held a brief ceremony on the bow presided over by Bill Surgi. Bill had taken a page from the Japanese book, having saved the flower leis we'd been given on Midway after finding the wreck. By some fateful coincidence, today was U.S. Memorial Day. It is hard to imagine a more appropriate moment to be saying farewell to the *Yorktown*.

Bill wore his aviation mechanic's uniform, standard-issue blue dungarees and the cap he had worn on the *Yorktown*. When he spoke of his fallen comrades, he removed the cap and put on his old steel helmet—his "tin hat"—the one that probably saved his life when the first airplane-launched torpedo hit, the hat he'd refused to leave behind when the *Yorktown* was abandoned.

He began by thanking the crew of the *Laney Chouest* and the Navy team, everyone who had joined together to find his old ship.

"Here lies my home for ten months," he continued, "in peace and war. Now that we have seen where she lies, let her lie still. My shipmates and I were here when a glorious page in our history was played out. We were doing our best. This helmet I wore at my battle station on June 4, 1942. Oh, yes, I do remember that day. And now I cast these petals on the water in memory of those who have gone before us."

As you can imagine, there weren't too many dry eyes on the foredeck.

Our discovery of the *Yorktown* meant more to Bill Surgi than to anyone else on board. He was especially disappointed when the memorial plaque (opposite) that we planned to set down on the flight deck broke free during its descent. After the discovery, we toasted him and his ship with champagne (above) and joined him in a ceremony of remembrance (right).

AND SO WE HEADED HOME VICTORIOUS, IN A MANNER OF SPEAKING. BUT VICTORY, IN PEACE as in war, is almost always bittersweet. At Midway in 1942 it came at the cost of many human lives, both American and Japanese, and untold suffering. At Midway in 1998 it came despite an unprecedented series of technical disasters. And the *Kaga* and the other Japanese carriers still lie undiscovered and unhonored.

The world has already saluted the discovery of the *Yorktown* as a triumph. I'm not so sure. But maybe it will help remind a new and younger generation of the remarkable sacrifices made by their elders on both sides of the wide Pacific and of the enduring truth that no victory in war can ever fully justify its human cost.

Chapter Eight
The Yorktown Today

GIVEN THAT SHE HAS SPENT 56 YEARS ON THE BOTTOM, the *Yorktown*'s state of preservation is surprising. So much of the ship is still recognizable, including the pilothouse, where the ship's binnacle is visible, and almost all of the wooden flight deck. The gun mounts and guns are in such good condition that some of the white rubber eyepieces on the 20 mm gunsights are still there. And except where intense heat damaged it, the original paint still covers the ship.

If the *Yorktown*'s preservation impressed us, it had a profound effect on those who had once called the ship home. When John Greenbacker saw the first picture of the pilothouse, he was immediately transported to the ship in the moments before Captain Buckmaster ordered her abandoned. "I could see the captain walking up and down on the outside walkway on the starboard side, agonizing about whether to order abandon ship," he told me. Bill Surgi's old shipmate, Gordon Skinner, joked that as soon as he saw pictures of the wreck, he thought about retrieving two mementos from his locker: the Bible his uncle had carried through World War I and a statue of the Buddha he had been given by a pilot friend.

The images we salvaged will almost surely be the only ones ever taken of this noble shipwreck. But given that there is little sediment in the open Pacific (maybe a centimeter will settle on the ship every thousand years), the *Yorktown* will look the way we found her for many, many years to come.

(Opposite) Ken Marschall's haunting painting of the sunken *Yorktown*.

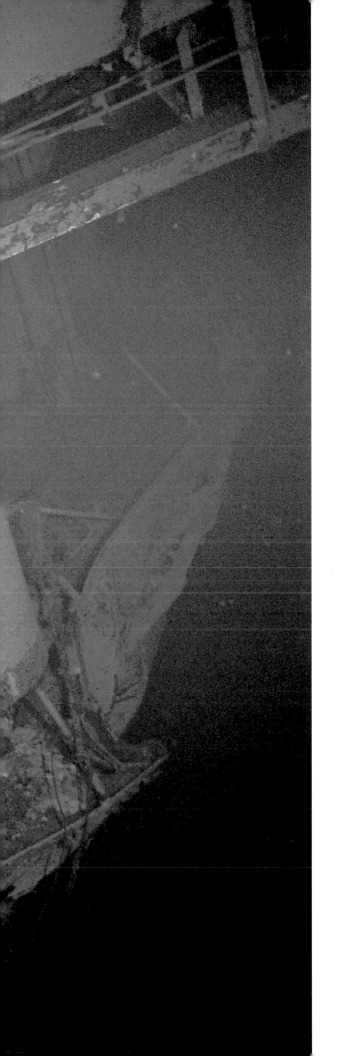

THE BOW

(Left) Two 20 mm guns still mounted on the ship's bow are readily recognizable in a 1942 photograph (right) shot from a slightly different angle.
(Above) The *Yorktown*'s identification numeral 5 can be made out on the battered port bow.
(Top) Behind the wire railing lies a fire hose, last used after the bomb attack on June 4, 1942.

(Next page) On the carrier's port side, the ATV peers into a large torpedo hole at the mudline.

THE GUNS

(Top left) The *Yorktown*'s forward port 20 mm guns are now gone. Once mounted as shown below, these weapons were jettisoned by salvage crews on June 6th during their attempts to lighten the ship and reduce her list. In contrast to these lighter guns,

all but one of the ship's 5-inch guns remain in place (bottom left and opposite), still trained outboard as if ready for use. Although a little battered, they look much as they did during the Battle of Midway (above).

THE BRIDGE

The most evocative area of the *Yorktown* wreck is the bridge and pilothouse (above and in period photograph, opposite). As we looked through the square, window-like ports and the open doors, it was easy to imagine what it was like when men stood by those windows scanning the sky or the flight deck below, and to picture Captain Buckmaster pacing anxiously before ordering that his ship be abandoned. Atop the pilothouse stands the now rather

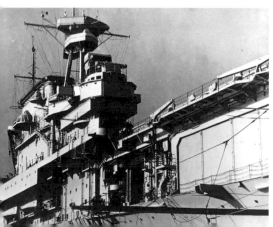

battered fire-control director, which relayed the range, bearing, and altitude of enemy targets to the ship's gunners. (Top) Below the larger windows of the charthouse can be seen the small rectangular windows of the *Yorktown*'s armored battle lookout. This lookout was intended to give some cover from shells and shrapnel during attack. (Above) The ship's bell mounted outside the wheelhouse, at upper left, provides a simple but poignant nautical touch.

THE CRANE

The *Yorktown*'s crane (opposite) still stands at the rear of the island but the arm that once hoisted planes and heavy cargo aboard, as seen in the period photograph at right, has since collapsed.

The wreck bristles with heavy machine guns like those (above) that still guard the roof of the pilothouse. (Below) A lone machine gun stands sentinel at the far port end of the bow.

(Above) Today the *Yorktown* lists nearly as sharply as it did after the torpedo hits on June 4, 1942 (left)—except that now the ship slopes to starboard, not port. In this view of the port side of the island, a doorway at bottom center that once led from the flight deck to the upper levels of the *Yorktown*'s island is clearly identical to the one in the shot of the listing ship at left. The knotted ropes visible in the older picture were thrown down from the still-intact catwalk to help men stationed high in the ship's island to reach the deck after the battle.

(Above) The searchlight platform still juts from the forward side of the island superstructure, just as it did in 1942 (left). Although the catwalk is in good shape, the steel below it has deteriorated badly, perhaps weakened by fires started by the bomb that tore through the decks and burst in the boiler uptakes.

(Next page) In a starboard-side view of the wreck, the ATV ventures into the mouth of the No. 1 elevator. All three of the elevators are open, probably because the lifts that once lowered the airplanes are in the down position.

THE STERN

(Right) In this dramatic shot of the stern, the embossed letters of the ship's name are faintly visible, even though they were painted over at the outbreak of war. The photograph (below)

shows the name as it originally appeared on the ship's stern in peacetime. Between the time of her commissioning and Midway, the *Yorktown* underwent numerous modifications. One major addition was the thick cables that run around the top edge of the hull. These are degaussing cables, intended to help neutralize the ship's magnetic charge. This, in turn, would help protect her from attack by magnetic mines and torpedoes.

Chapter Nine
Leaving Midway

Tuesday, May 26, 1998

IDWAY HAS GONE BACK TO THE BIRDS—THE "GOONEY BIRDS," TO BE precise. That's what the servicemen called the Laysan albatrosses that breed on the atoll. They even named the Midway newspaper the *Gooney Gazette*. Back in 1942, the birds had been pushed aside by men and flying machines. Harry Ferrier says he hardly remembers seeing any when he was there then. Now there are so many albatrosses—roughly 800,000 nesting birds—on these two tiny islands that it's only safe for airplanes to land and take off at night. (Midway is home to 70 percent of the total world population of Laysan albatrosses.) Our flight for Honolulu leaves after dark, so my last look at Midway will be of a few scattered lights twinkling in the tropical night. I'll never see it as the fliers did in 1942, two tiny green islands, the smaller one crisscrossed with runways, ringed by white foam from the coral reef, and set against a deep Pacific blue.

(Opposite) On Midway today, nature is reclaiming the islands. But it is still possible to find reminders of World War II, such as this three-inch gun.

Sitting on a deserted beach facing an empty sea—as I am doing this afternoon while making this final entry in my personal log of our Midway expedition—I really do feel midway between nowhere and nowhere. If I look out to the horizon, where the blue ocean meets the blue sky, I can imagine that I'm suspended in a vastness outside space and time. A lot like Midway itself. Except for a brief moment 56 years ago, Midway has been a cul-de-sac, a backwater, an afterthought—outside history, a place where not much happened or was ever likely to.

It's a strange and magical spot, this—more like a centuries-old archaeological site than a modern-era battlefield. These days, the forces of nature—with a helping hand from the United States Fish and Wildlife Service—are returning Midway to its natural

state. Relatively little remains of the once-bustling airbase that, at its peak in June 1942, was home to thousands of men, but what does remain is hauntingly evocative: gun emplacements; bunkers; the original seaplane hangar, half-destroyed in the battle; and the runway on which Bert Earnest and Harry Ferrier crash-landed their shot-up Grumman Avenger. The runway is overgrown with vegetation and dotted with bird nests, gradually fading away. The whole atoll may be turning into a wildlife reserve, but the reminders of the Battle of Midway will never disappear. I'm sure that the ecology-minded tourists who travel thousands of miles to look at birds will leave with much more than memories of breeding albatrosses, unspoiled beaches, and delicious French food. I'm sure they will leave with a sense of wonder about Midway's moment, when this small isolated island sat at the center of history.

Built for an invasion that never came, a cement pillbox stands sentinel at twilight on a Midway beach.

For those of us who have just returned to land, the ghosts of 1942 are everywhere. We're still living with one foot in the past and one in the here and now, part of our minds still three miles beneath the sea as we walk on the *Yorktown*'s listing flight deck one last time before finally abandoning for good the ship we love, the other part thinking about tonight's farewell dinner—about homes and families and plans. In a few days I'll be back in Connecticut with Barbara and the kids, back to everyday life.

I wonder what the world will think of our discovery. It made the newspapers and the nightly newscasts, but will it quickly be forgotten—a curiosity from a piece of the past that people growing up today don't understand or care about? The search for the *Yorktown* was perhaps my biggest gamble ever, my biggest roll of the dice—using unfamiliar technology to look for the deepest wreck I have ever hunted. But our travails at sea will fade fast. What people will remember, if anything, will be the ship and what she meant. And still means.

Just why do we go to all the trouble of looking for these lost ships? And why does the world seem to care? Maybe part of what we do by bringing deep shipwrecks to light is to hold up a mirror to the present, a mirror whose reflection shows us ourselves in the past—and shows us the past in the present. If that makes any sense. The physical presence of a *Titanic*, a *Bismarck*, a *Yorktown* causes us to relive history in a way that history books can never make us do. Does a discovery like this help us learn from our parents' and grandparents' mistakes? I don't know. But it does show us that we can't run away from the truth; it has a way of catching up with us.

Whatever else we can say about our return to Midway, we have now become a part of its story. The battle didn't end in June 1942. It lived on through the friends and relatives to whom the veterans told their experiences. Then the historians began to write about it. Our discovery has merely added a chapter to the book of Midway, connected us to a great historical moment.

I wonder how this latest chapter will affect four of its main characters: Yuji Akamatsu, Haruo Yoshino, Harry Ferrier, and Bill Surgi. Each of them seems to have found in an empty patch of ocean some sense of completion—even if we didn't find a Japanese ship for Yuji and Haruo or an American airplane for Harry. How will it affect those Navy boys who so stubbornly fought our technology battles and finally won? Their parents weren't even born when their Navy met the Japanese fleet at Midway. And how will it affect somebody like our video tech Jay Minkin, a guy with no connection to this place, who had never even heard of Midway before we invited him to come along? As the expedition unfolded, I could see his eyes opening and his brain becoming more and more curious. By the end he realized that this was far more than just an unusual video gig. By setting sail with us, he was part of something with meaning.

The meaning of Midway—its precise place in the history of naval warfare, its

significance for the war in the Pacific—continues to be a field of debate. Historians will be arguing about it for a long time yet, but there's no question that the battle was big and its consequences far-reaching. Whether it was the turning point of the war in the Pacific, as many have claimed, it certainly made that war shorter. A Japanese victory might have delayed the inevitable but could hardly have prevented America from prevailing in the end. There is no question that the battle gave convincing proof of the supremacy of the aircraft carrier as an instrument of naval warfare, a supremacy it still retains. Only the advent of nuclear-powered submarines armed with missiles has even threatened the aircraft carrier's strategic dominance.

More germane to our present enterprise, what does a shipwreck add to our understanding of a historical event? I suppose the simple act of discovery gives the event a physical immediacy that forces us to consider it afresh. Just seeing the name *Yorktown* in raised letters on her stern and her painted number 5 (she was America's fifth aircraft carrier) brings her into the present. Certainly, our discovery adds some interesting details, some illuminating footnotes. In the case of the *Yorktown*, we were able, from examining a wreck, to embellish the story of how and why she sank. We now know, for example, that the ship went down in one piece, and there is strong evidence that it went down stern first, as suggested by the action reports of the escorting destroyers, since the stern is deeper in the bottom. The condition of the wreck confirms some of the details of the *Yorktown*'s battle: the torpedo damage in the port side, the bomb hole in the flight deck just aft of the midships elevator, the fire in the boiler uptakes.

Maybe our discovery of the wreck will help rectify an omission by the wartime U.S. Navy. Talking to Bill Surgi and other veterans of the *Yorktown*, I have learned that there is a deep and abiding sense of collective grievance that their ship was never awarded a unit citation for its gallant service. At the time, I suppose, there was a sense that you can't honor a ship that is abandoned and then sinks—and a belief that this one could and should have been salvaged. We have enough distance now to realize that what is really most remarkable about the *Yorktown* is how long she lasted and what a stubborn fight she put up. The *Yorktown* is not a symbol of failure; she is a symbol of not giving up in the face of great difficulty. She and her men deserve the recognition too long denied.

To those who sailed on her, the *Yorktown* was more than a large piece of machinery, amazingly complex but ultimately lifeless. She was their home—a happy ship, a community that worked, a place they knew and loved. When I think of all those young men—boys, really—who lived on board her for a few years, or merely months, she becomes a symbol of innocence. Innocence sacrificed. Such sacrifice can be tolerable only if it is remembered and honored.

Somehow it seems right that the last words in my log should belong to one of our four veterans, Yuji Akamatsu: "I've always wanted to come here to comfort the spirits of my fallen comrades, but I never had the chance to do so. As a result of being asked to be part of this expedition, I was able to come here. I'm extremely grateful for that. The first thing I would want to say to my dead comrades is 'May your spirits rest in peace.'"

The Midway lagoon contains many vestiges of battle, including (opposite) the wreckage of an airplane, most likely an American one, lost defending the island on June 4, and a machine gun (above).

(Next page) A lovingly restored lone Dauntless is silhouetted by the setting sun.

Acknowledgments

NO EXPLORER DOES IT ALL ON HIS OWN. AS ALWAYS, I AM INDEBTED TO far more people than I could ever name in a list. To Cathy Offinger, who has been with me on so many trips before, thanks again. Thanks to National Geographic, which has been there since the beginning, with special thanks to David Doubilet, Mark Thiessen, and Keith Morehead for their great efforts in documenting the expedition and discovery of the *Yorktown*. Thanks to Bruce Appelgate, Karen Sender, and the rest of the sonar team from the University of Hawaii. Thanks also to Comdr. Kurt Sadorf, Lt. Jay Dryer, Chief David Swarm, and the other members of the Navy crew who worked so hard to keep the Advanced Tethered Vehicle going, often under a lot of pressure (some of it applied by me, I'm afraid). And thanks also to another Navy man, Erick Murray. Thanks to the captain and crew of the *Laney Chouest* and Dave Mindell of MIT. Thanks above all to Yuji Akamatsu, Haruo Yoshino, Harry Ferrier, and Bill Surgi, for sharing what were, I know, sometimes painful memories, and for helping to bring that faraway battle alive. Finally, thanks to Barbara, and to my children, Douglas, Ben and Emily Rose, for putting up with the absences that are part of exploring. To anyone I may have overlooked, my heartfelt apologies.

Robert D. Ballard

Rick Archbold would like to thank Chuck Haberlein and Robert J. Cressman of the Naval Historical Center in Washington, D.C., and John Lundstrom of the Milwaukee Public Museum, three fine historians without whom *Return to Midway* would not have been possible. They directed me to essential sources, read and commented on every word of text, and helped steer me clear of the shoals of historical error. I'd like to single out John Lundstrom for special thanks. From the moment I first contacted him, he supported our Midway project with incredible gusto. His love of his subject and his willingness to share his knowledge are a credit to his profession. He never tired of my unending questions and saved me from many factual errors. Those mistakes that undoubtedly remain are my own.

Nor could this book exist without the help of a number of veterans of the battle, especially the four men who joined Dr. Ballard's Midway expedition: Yuji Akamatsu, Haruo Yoshino, Harry Ferrier, and Bill Surgi. Our Japanese translator, Junko Taguchi, acted as an able intermediary between me and our two Japanese veterans. A number of other Midway veterans spoke to me either by phone or e-mail (or both): Pete Newberg (secretary of the U.S.S. *Yorktown* Association); John Miller; Gordon Skinner; Sid Flum; John Greenbacker; Thomas E. Allen; Captain Vane Bennett; Admiral William Leonard; Bert Earnest. I also drew on previously conducted interviews with Takeshi Maeda and Taisuke Maruyama.

The following participants in the 1998 expedition helped me flesh out the story of the search and discovery: Cathy Offinger (who never lets me down); Dave Mindell; Bruce Appelgate; Karen Sender; Jay Minkin; Peter Schnall; and Neil Conan of National Public Radio.

Peter Schnall and Denise Williams at Partisan Pictures provided interview transcripts, biographical material, and much support.

Tom Allen, who covered the expedition for NATIONAL GEOGRAPHIC, wrote excellent dispatches and kindly directed me to valuable source material.

Help with specific questions came from: Mark E. Horan; and Robert Shallenberger and Nancy Hoffman of the Midway Atoll National Wildlife Refuge.

Special thanks to Torontonian Brett Matos, who found and returned a lost briefcase full of Midway material at a crucial early stage of the writing. And finally the usual kudos to the crack editorial and production team at Madison Press Books, who provided superb support every inch of the way: editorial director Hugh Brewster; dauntless editor and photo sleuth Ian Coutts; patient copy editor Alison Reid; and tireless production coordinator Sandra Hall.

Madison Press Books would like to thank Richard Olsenius, Kevin Craig, and Brendan McCabe at National Geographic and the various expedition photographers, David Doubilet, Mark Thiessen, Keith Morehead, and Glen Marullo, for their invaluable, and beautiful, record of the search and discovery; Cathy Offinger of the Institute for Exploration and the Woods Hole Oceanographic Institute for carefully checking the manuscript and providing invaluable reference material on the underwater expedition.

Thanks to Laurie Vigneault of The Greenwich Workshop for helping hunt down appropriate paintings for the book; thanks to the painters whose work appears herein—William S. Phillips, Craig Kodera, Alfred Leete, Ken Marschall, and Stan Stokes; thanks to Chuck Haberlein, Dave Manning, and Ed Finney at the Naval Historical Center and Gail Munro of the Navy Art Gallery; Bill T. Barr, former U.S.S. *Enterprise* photographer, and Bill Roy, who did the same job aboard *Yorktown*, and Pete Montalvo, another old *Yorktown* hand; thanks to Peter Schnall of Partisan Pictures for the loan of so many historic photographs. Thanks also to Mark E. Horan, keeper of the Torpedo Eight flame, as well as to Hill Goodspeed, curator of the Naval Aviation Museum in Pensacola, Florida, and Dean Clatterbuck and Bob Anderson of the Naval Security Group.

Bibliography

Bradford, James C., ed. *Quarterdeck and Bridge: Two Centuries of American Naval Leaders.* Annapolis: Naval Institute Press, 1997.

Buell, Thomas B. *The Quiet Warrior: A Biography of Admiral Raymond A. Spruance.* Boston: Little Brown & Co., 1974.

Buell, Harold L. *Dauntless Helldivers: A Dive-Bomber Pilot's Epic Story of the Carrier Battles.* New York: Orion Books, 1986.

Collier, Basil. *Japanese Aircraft of World War II.* London: Sidgwick and Jackson, 1979.

Cressman, Robert J. *That Gallant Ship: USS Yorktown (CV 5).* Missoula, Montana: Pictorial Histories, 1985.

Cressman et al. *A Glorious Day in our History: The Battle of Midway, 4-6 June 1942.* Missoula, Montana: Pictorial Histories, 1990.

Earnest, Albert K., and Harry H. Ferrier. "Avengers at Midway," *Foundation,* Spring 1996.

Ferrier, Harry H. "Torpedo Squadron Eight, The Other Chapter," *U.S. Naval Institute Proceedings,* October 1964.

Fuchida, Mitsuo, and Masatake Okuyima. *Midway: The Battle that Doomed Japan.* Annapolis: Naval Institute Press, 1955.

Gay, George H. *Sole Survivor.* Naples, Florida: Privately printed, 1979.

Keegan, John. *The Price of Admiralty: War at Sea from Man of War to Submarine.* London: Hutchinson, 1988.

Layton, Edwin T., with Roger Pineau and John Costello. *And I Was There: Pearl Harbor and Midway—Breaking the Secrets.* New York: William Morrow, 1985.

Lord, Walter. *Incredible Victory.* New York: Harper & Row, 1967.

Lundstrom, John B. *The First South Pacific Campaign: Pacific Fleet Strategy, December 1941-June 1942.* Annapolis: Naval Institute Press, 1976.

_____. *The First Team: Pacific Naval Air Combat from Pearl Harbor to Midway.* Annapolis: Naval Institute Press, 1976.

_____. "Frank Jack Fletcher Got a Bum Rap," *Naval History,* Summer 1992.

Mason, Theodore C. *Battleship Sailor.* Annapolis: Naval Institute Press, 1982.

Mears, Frederick C. *Carrier Combat.* New York: Doubleday Doran, 1944.

Morison, Samuel Eliot. *Coral Sea, Midway, and Submarine Actions, May 1942-August 1942,* Vol. IV in *History of United States Naval Operations in World War II.* Boston: Little Brown, 1950.

Polmar, Norman. *Aircraft Carriers.* New York: Doubleday, 1969.

Prado, John. *Combined Fleet Decoded: The Secret History of American Intelligence and the Japanese Navy in World War II.* New York: Random House, 1995.

Prange, Gordon W., with Donald M. Goldstein and Katherine V. Dillon. *Miracle at Midway.* New York: McGraw-Hill, 1982.

Regan, Stephen. *In Bitter Tempest: The Biography of Admiral Frank Jack Fletcher.* Ames: Iowa State University Press, 1994.

Smith, William W. *Midway: Turning Point of the Pacific.* New York: Thomas Y. Crowell, 1966.

Swanborough, Gordon, and Peter M. Bowers. *United States Naval Aircraft Since 1911.* Annapolis: Naval Institute Press, 1976.

Tillman, Barrett. *The Dauntless Dive Bomber in World War II.* Annapolis: Naval Institute Press, 1976.

U.S. Navy, Office of Naval Intelligence. *The Japanese Story of the Battle of Midway.* Washington, D.C.: GPO, 1947. (Translation of parts of the First Air Fleet, Detailed Battle Report No. 6, Midway Operations, 27 May-9 June 1942, in the *ONI Review,* May 1947.)

van der Vat, Dan. *The Pacific Campaign: World War II, the U.S.-Japanese Naval War, 1941-1945.* New York: Simon & Schuster, 1991.

Wilmott, H. P. *The Barrier and the Javelin: Japanese and Allied Strategies, February to June 1942.* Annapolis: Naval Institute Press, c.1983.

Photograph and Illustration Credits

Index

References to photographs are indicated by italicized page numbers

DESIGN AND ART DIRECTION
Gordon Sibley Design Inc.

EDITORIAL DIRECTOR
Hugh M. Brewster

PROJECT EDITOR
Ian R. Coutts

EDITORIAL ASSISTANCE
Susan Aihoshi, Wanda Nowakowska, Alison Reid

PRODUCTION DIRECTOR
Susan Barrable

PRODUCTION COORDINATOR
Sandra L. Hall

PAINTINGS
Craig Kodera, Alfred Leete, Ken Marschall, William S. Phillips, Stan Stokes

MAPS AND DIAGRAMS
Jack McMaster

COLOR SEPARATION
Colour Technologies

PRINTING AND BINDING
Butler & Tanner Limited

Return to Midway was produced by Madison Press Books,

which is under the direction of Albert E. Cummings